GREAT MISSIONARIES

OF

THE CHURCH

JOHN COLERIDGE PATTESON.

GREAT MISSIONARIES

OF

THE CHURCH

BY

THE REV. CHARLES C. CREEGAN

AND

MRS. JOSEPHINE A. B. GOODNOW

WITH AN INTRODUCTION BY THE

REV. FRANCIS E. CLARK

Essay Index Reprint Series

 BOOKS FOR LIBRARIES PRESS
FREEPORT, NEW YORK

First Published 1895
Reprinted 1972

Library of Congress Cataloging in Publication Data

Creegan, Charles Cole, 1850-1939.
    Great missionaries of the church.

    (Essay index reprint series)
    Reprint of the 1895 ed.
    1. Missionaries. I. Goodnow, Josephine A. B.,
joint author. II. Title.
BV3700.C67 1972   266'.00922   73-37522
ISBN 0-8369-2541-6

PRINTED IN THE UNITED STATES OF AMERICA
BY
NEW WORLD BOOK MANUFACTURING CO., INC.
HALLANDALE, FLORIDA 33009

TO

The Young People of Our Day,

THIS VOLUME

Is AFFECTIONATELY DEDICATED.

PREFACE.

THE admirable Introduction to this volume, from the pen of my friend, the Rev. Francis E. Clark, D.D., makes a formal preface unnecessary. I wish, however, to acknowledge the kindness of those who have made this book possible by their timely aid.

My best thanks are due to the proprietors of that excellent Christian paper, *The Congregationalist*, in whose columns eight of these sketches have already appeared, for permission to republish them, together with fifteen others, in permanent form. As a fitting recognition of the invaluable aid I have received from Mrs. Josephine A. B. Goodnow of Dubuque, Iowa, her name has been placed on the title page.

I have also received valuable assistance in the matter of data, and in other ways, from Mrs. Mary E. Logan, late missionary in Micronesia; Miss Clementine Butler, Newton Centre, Mass.; the Rev. James Mudge, Lowell, Mass., late associate of Bishop Thoburn in India; the Rev. Ross Taylor, New York; and Mr. James D. Creegan of Brooklyn.

I wish also to acknowledge many courtesies from the publishers at whose suggestion the book has been prepared, and who have, through their artistic and mechanical work, left nothing to be desired.

The reader will miss the names of some famous missionaries of this century; but the plan of the book will be seen, when it is observed that we have representatives from seven denominations and sixteen mission lands. To include all the missionary heroes of our time would require several volumes.

If these sketches help to deepen sympathy for missions, and to increase gifts to the cause, and if they may be the means of leading some of our young people to follow the example of these noble men, who have given their all to build up Christ's Kingdom, they will have fully answered the purpose for which they are now sent forth.

C. C. C.

BIBLE HOUSE, NEW YORK,
May 10, 1895.

INTRODUCTION.

I CAN scarcely conceive of a more useful book for young people to own and study than this most interesting volume of missionary biography.

If it is a vitally necessary thing for young Christians who would develop the most intelligent type of religious character to know the lives of the apostles of old, and to become familiar with their acts as recorded by the pen of inspiration, it is scarcely less important that they should study the later and no less thrilling acts of later apostles of the church.

In this volume the acts of the apostles are continued in graphic and interesting chapters. Young people everywhere, whatever their age or sex (for there is many a young man and woman with heart fresh

and unfurrowed, though the brow may be
wrinkled by three-score years and ten),
enjoy stirring adventures, lively incidents,
and heroic stories.

No less interesting to every healthy
mind is a well-written biography, a story
which tells of the actual hopes and fears
and joys and acts of a living man. This
volume combines the excellences of the
spirited story of adventure, and the graphic
biography of real men and women. What
more happy combination could be found?
The biography in almost every case is a
story of adventure; the story of adventure
is a biography — a life history of some
great man or woman.

After having taken a long journey
through many missionary lands, my delib-
erate and often recorded opinion has been
that, if we seek for heroes to-day, we will
find them, for the most part, on missionary
soil. Not that many a humble, inconspicu-
ous life is not lived most heroically at
home. I would not belittle with a single
adjective of faint praise the splendid devo-

tion of humble Christians. But if we are speaking of conspicuous heroism, of lives which God has marked as eminent examples to the world, we must look for them very largely on the frontier of our own land where our home missionaries have gone, or in the dark nations of the world to which our foreign missionaries are carrying the light of gospel truth.

I am glad to record again that missionary work in all the various Protestant denominations, in all parts of the world, is, in my eyes, the most promising and hopeful feature of modern civilization. For the enlargement of commerce, for the spread of civilization, for the uplifting of humanity, for the redemption of the world, there is no such force as that which is exerted by the Anglo-Saxon missionaries of the cross, the ministers of the Lord Jesus Christ.

If this opinion is true of the average missionary to-day, at work in the foreign field, and I believe it is, how doubly true is it of the great missionaries of the

church, Patteson and Carey and Neesima
and Williams and Taylor and Livingstone.

It only remains to be said that this most
interesting subject is treated by its authors
in a way worthy of their theme. With this
book in his hands, no one can say that missionary biography is dull, stale, and unin-
teresting. No one will yawn over insipid
pages, or read only from a sense of duty
these charming chapters. If more light
and more knowledge are the great pre-
requisites for larger interests and larger
gifts, then I believe that this volume will
do not a little to kindle to a brighter flame
the interest of Christians in missionary
themes.

Already the fire has begun to blaze in
many a young heart. In a multitude of
young people's conventions no theme to-
day is so interesting as the missionary
theme. No subjects so stir the hearts
and quicken the pulses of a host of young
disciples as those connected with the winning of the world to Christ. This book
will supply the fire of enthusiasm with the

one fuel that is needed — the fuel of information.

If this result is accomplished, then the missionary treasuries will feel the influence of this book. To some extent the mountainous debt should be scaled down, and the treasuries, refilled as this volume goes from family to family on its blessed mission of information and inspiration.

FRANCIS E. CLARK.

BOSTON, *April* 8, 1895.

CONTENTS.

I.

JOHN COLERIDGE PATTESON.

BORN APRIL 1, 1827, DIED SEPT. 20, 1871.

GREAT MISSIONARIES

OF

THE CHURCH.

I.

BISHOP PATTESON.

THE lives of some men are an atmosphere into which we cannot enter without feeling braced and invigorated. Such was the life of John Coleridge Patteson, possessing as it did the attributes of real manhood, unswerving allegiance to right, and a human tenderness. The poor heathen, for whose sake he gave up all, were the most unpromising material to be found in the wide world for conversion into citizens of the kingdom of heaven. But the faith of Patteson was constantly strengthened by witnessing the spiritual beauty and fidelity of those who in due time sat at the feet of Christ, clothed and in their right mind.

John Coleridge Patteson was born on April 1, 1827. His father, John Patteson, was a lawyer of no mean repute. His mother was of the Coleridge family, and her line was distinguished by the philosopher, Samuel Taylor Coleridge. To the future bishop she gave her family name; and to those who knew him best, not only as a boy, but afterwards when he had reached man's estate, he was known as "Coley." Consideration for others, kindness· and sweetness of nature, were his leading characteristics.

While at Eton he was profoundly impressed by a farewell sermon which Bishop Selwyn preached in October, 1841, at Windsor, where the bishop had acted as curate. When calling on his mother to bid her farewell, that eminent prelate and missionary said, with a kind of prophetic anticipation, "Lady Patteson, will you give me Coley?" and the boy said he would

like some time to go with the bishop.
Meantime his school-life was arduous and
successful. At Oxford, where he entered
with deep interest into the religious move-
ments of the day, he obtained, in 1849,
a classical second class, and subsequently
a fellowship.

His examination for his degree was followed by a tour in Germany and Italy. In
1853 he was ordained, and took the curacy
of Alfington. Here his sweet manner and
musical voice helped to win the hearts of
his people; but general society he never
liked, small talk he declared he could not
manufacture, and morning callers were the
plague of his life.

On the 19th of August, 1854, he joined
in welcoming the bishop of New Zealand,
who came to visit England after twelve
years of work, during which he had
founded his church, organized its government, and planned his system of missionary aggression on the five groups of
islands which he combined under the col-
lective name of Melanesia. As early
as 1848 Bishop Selwyn had visited these

islands ; and he soon perceived that it was
vain to think of dealing with them by
planting a resident English clergyman in
each of them. He also believed that no
church could take effectual root without
a native clergy; and he accordingly determined upon the plan to bring boys
from the islands to New Zealand, to edu-
cate them there in St. John's College, and
then send them home to become teachers
of their countrymen.

But what was now necessary was a man
who should be able to " rough it " among
the islands, and yet take up with spirit
and ability the education and training of
the islanders themselves. In quest of
such help Bishop Selwyn visited England
again, and now followed up the thought
of 1841, by asking Sir John Patteson,
" Will you give me Coley? " His words
fell upon a mind in the young man himself already charged with the subject; and
in March, 1855, he left, his villagers de-
ploring his departure, and sailed for New
Zealand.

Here he wrought earnestly in the schools

until 1860, when, despite his modest reluctance, he obeyed the earnest requisition
of Bishop Selwyn, and agreed to undertake
the episcopal office. In this year, 1860,
he assumed the direction of the Melane-
sian mission, and founded a mission-house
at Mota. He was consecrated bishop on
February 24; and from this time for ten
and a half years remained in sole charge of
the missions of the Church in the islands.
Lady Martin gives the following brief description of the consecration service : " I
shall never forget the expression of his
face as he knelt in the quaint rocket. It
was meek and calm and holy, as though
all conflict was over, and he was resting
in divine strength. It was altogether a
wonderful scene — the three consecrating
bishops, all noble-looking men, the goodly
number of clergy, and Hohna's fine, intelligent, brown face among them, and then
the long line of island boys and of St.
Stephen's native teachers and their wives,
— all living testimonies of mission-work."
Bishop Patteson was now formally in-

stalled in the chapel of St. Andrew as head of the college. Miss Yonge says : " It was in his private classes that he exercised such wonderful influence, his musical voice, his holy face, his gentle manner, all helping to impress and draw even the dullest."

Putting down his natural fastidiousness, he gave dignity to the very humblest of his duties. Some idea of his many-sidedness may be had from the following letter : " I can hardly tell you how much I regret not knowing something about the treatment of simple surgical cases. If I had studied the practical, bled, drawn teeth, mixed medicines, it would have been worth something. Many trades need not be attempted ; but every missionary ought to be a carpenter, a mason, something of a butcher, and a good deal of a cook."

The incessant labors and occasional dangers of his life were relieved by his vivid interest in his work, and by his enjoyment of a climate which was to him highly genial. The spirit of fun, which had had free play in his boyhood, did not depart from him during his episcopate, and it found fittest openings in the innocent festivities among the natives. He taught them to play cricket. They showed a marvellous eagerness for knowledge, and labored like the smallest English children at the mysteries of the alphabet. Patteson could not bring himself to consider the poor, unenlightened heathen as under special condemnation ; rather, he rejoiced in hope of the glory of God fulfilled in them when the light of the gospel shall shine in their hearts. He was a believer in the love of God.

Early in 1870 Bishop Patteson was struck down by a severe and dangerous attack of internal inflammation, and it was evident that his unremitted exertion was carrying him with great rapidity into an early old age. With darkened countenance, and frame prematurely bowed, he went to Auckland for advice. His ailment was declared chronic, but not necessarily fatal. He began to be aware that there must be a change in the amount and character of his work. He says : —

"I think I shall have to forego some of the more risky and adventurous part of the work in the islands. I don't mean that I shall not take the voyages, and stop about on the islands as before ; but I must do it all more carefully, and avoid much that of old I never thought about."

He mended very slowly ; but he determined to return to Melanesia. He completed his circuit of the islands in October, and, arriving at Norfolk Island, resumed his old mapping of the day for teaching, study, and devotion, never forgetting correspondence in its turn. He worked " from before 5 A.M. till soon after 9 P.M., when I go off to bed quite tired. I am very seldom alone. I may do a great deal of work yet, rather in a quieter way than of old."

His mind continued to act, however, with unabated interest upon all portions of his work, and also upon Hebrew philologically viewed, upon the events of the year at Rome and on the French frontier, and upon theology. On April 27, 1871, he set out for his closing voyage. At Mota, the missionary headquarters, he recognized a great progress. Christianity had so far become a power and habit of life, that he felt warranted, notwithstanding all his strictness about the administration of baptism, in giving that sacrament to young children. After quite a visit at Fiji, he leaves there, having baptized 289 persons, and visits other groups of islands. His experience is generally pleasant, but it is checkered by rumors of crime and retaliation for crime in connection with the labor traffic. Returning to Mota, he makes record of a concourse of people flocking to be taught. " I sleep on a table ; people under and around me."

Such was the nightly preparation of the invalid for his long, laborious, uncomplaining days. On August 6 we have several thoughtful pages on difficulties of theology : " How thankful I am that I am far away from the noise and worry of this sceptical yet earnest age."

Sailing on the 20th, he sends to Bishop

Abraham an interesting summary of the state of things at Mota. The bishops, his brethren in New Zealand, jointly urged him to go to England; but he declined. The slave traffic still casts a dark shadow across his path. "I hear that a vessel has gone to Santa Cruz; and I must be very cautious there, for there has been some disturbance almost to a certainty." On September 16 he finds himself off the Santa Cruz group: "I pray God that if it be his will, and if it be the appointed time, he may enable us in his own way to begin some little work among these very wild but energetic islanders. I am fully alive to the probability that some outrage has been committed here by one or more vessels. I am quite aware that we may be exposed to considerable risk on this account, but I don't think there is very much cause for fear; first, because at these reef islands they know me very well, though they don't understand as yet our object in coming to them, and they may very easily connect us white people with the other white people who have ill-treated them. Still, I think if any violence has been used to the natives to the north face of the large island, Santa Cruz, I shall hear of it, and so be forewarned."

Accordingly, to Nukapu he went. Four canoes were seen hovering about the coral reef which surrounded the island. The vessel had to feel her way; so, lest the men in the canoes should be perplexed, he ordered the boat to be lowered, and when asked to go into one of the native boats, he did it to disarm suspicion, and was carried off toward the shore. The boat from the schooner could not get over the reef. The bishop was seen to land on the shore, and was then seen alive no more. After a while Mr. Atkin was struck with an arrow-head from the islanders in the canoe; but, in spite of suffering and weakness, he crossed the reef to seek the bishop. A canoe drifted toward them; the body of a man was seen as if crouching in it. They came up with it, and lifted the bundle wrapped in matting into the boat; two

words passed, "The body." Then it was
lifted up and laid across the skylight. The
placid smile was still on the face; there
was a palm-leaf fastened over the breast,
and when the mat was opened there were
five wounds.

This is an almost certain indication that
his death was vengeance for five of the
natives. " Blood for blood " is a sacred
law almost of nature wherever Christianity
has not prevailed, and a whole tribe is held
responsible for one. Five men in Fiji are
known to have been stolen from Nukapu;
and probably their families believed them
to have been killed, and believed themselves to be performing a sacred duty when
they dipped their weapons in the blood of
the bishop, whom they did not know well
enough to understand him to be their pro-
tector.

The next morning the body of John
Coleridge Patteson was committed to the
waters of the Pacific, Joseph Atkin, reading the burial service, even though then
recognizing his own sign of doom in a

body stiffened from a poisonous arrow which caused his death.

No summary can do justice to the character and career of Bishop Patteson. In him were singularly combined the spirit of chivalry, the glorious ornament of a bygone time; the spirit of charity, rare in every age; and the spirit of reverence. It is hardly possible to read the significant but modest record of his sacrifices, his labors, his perils, and his cares, without being vividly reminded of St. Paul, the prince and model of all missionary laborers, without feeling that the apostolic pattern is not even now without its imitators, and that the copy in this case recalls the original. The three highest titles that can be given to man are those of martyr, hero, saint; and which of the three is there that in substance it would be irrational to attach to the name of John Coleridge Patteson?

II.

TITUS COAN, MISSIONARY TO HAWAII.

BORN FEB. 1, 1801; DIED DEC. 1, 1882.

TITUS COAN.

II.

A BELT of island coast-line extending from north to south a hundred miles, and from one to three miles wide, dotted with groves and seamed by deep mountain chasms and scoriaceous lava-fields, varied by plains and hills of pasture-land, upon which feed herds of wild cattle — a land inhabited by 15,000 natives, grouped in villages of two or more hundred people, vicious, shameless, yet tractable, slaves to their chiefs, and herding together like animals — to this parish, occupying the eastern third of the island of Hawaii, was sent in 1835 the young missionary, Titus Coan.

In the town of Killingworth, Conn., he was born of old New England stock, Feb. 1, 1801. His boyhood was passed upon his father's farm, and he attended the

19

village schools.   Later he went to a military school; after this was employed as a
teacher in Western New York; and in
1831, through the influence of his cousin,
the Rev. Asahel Nettleton, he entered the
theological seminary at Auburn.   While
Mr. Coan was in the seminary he gave
much time to revival effort, and success
attended his labors.   He was licensed to
preach April 17, 1833.   On Aug. 16,
1833, he was sent to Patagonia by the
American Board, accompanied by the Rev.
Mr. Arms; and for four months they made
an earnest but unsuccessful attempt to
communicate to the ferocious nomads
something of their message.   The savages threatened them with death; and it
was only by stratagem that they made
their escape, and boarded a chance vessel, and returned to New London, Conn.,
in May, 1834.

Mr. Coan had been unable to receive
any communication from his family or
from his *fiancée*, Miss Fidelia Church,
during his absence; and the uncertainty

of his fate had been the source of the
deepest anxiety to them. After this trial
came the joy of reunion, which was celebrated by the marriage of Mr. Coan and
Miss Church on Nov. 3, 1834.

On December 5 they embarked at Boston for Honolulu. At that time the Hawaiian Islands seemed at the very ends of
the earth, and the trip was a six months'
voyage around Cape Horn. Neither Mr.
Coan nor his bride then had any idea
of returning to their native land. They
arrived at Honolulu, June 6, 1835, and
were welcomed by the missionaries then
assembled at their annual meeting. The
field in which Mr. Coan was to labor was
Hilo — now a thriving town, then in almost absolute retirement; and for many
years after his arrival there were no roads,
no bridges, and no horses in Hilo, and
Mr. Coan was obliged to make his tours
on foot. Mr. and Mrs. Coan were delighted that their future home was to be
upon the beautiful bay of Hilo, called after
the visit of Admiral Byron, Byron's Bay,

and adorned with the cocoa-palm, whose
lofty plumes rustled in the fresh sea-breeze.

Upon reaching the island, Mr. Coan
found several schools established by the
different missionaries, and that about one-
fourth of the natives could read. There
were a few hopeful converts, and a little
church of thirty-six members. Mr. Lyman
and his wife were then on the ground,
having settled at Hilo in 1832 ; and there
they remained until the death of Mr. Lyman in 1884, after an unbroken residence
of fifty-two years. They had charge of a
boarding-school, and much labor at the
home station ; while to Mr. Coan, robust
in health and a fervid speaker, the preaching and the touring were naturally assigned. In three months' time he began
to speak in the native tongue ; and before
the year closed he had made the circuit
of the island by canoe and on foot, a
trip of 300 miles. He preached forty-
three times in eight days, examined twenty
schools, and more than 1,200 scholars ;
conversed personally with multitudes, and

ministered to many sick persons, for he was something of a physician. He had at that time a daily school of ninety teachers, and Mrs. Coan one of 140 children.

In 1835 Mr. Coan said, " I have literally no leisure so much as to eat, finding myself constrained to preach, at times, twice before breakfast." During his tours through the island in 1836, the natives rallied in masses to hear Mr. Coan preach. The blind were led ; the maimed, the aged, and invalids were brought on the backs of their friends. Among the converts was the high priest of the volcano. He had been an idolater, a drunkard, and a murderer ; but he became penitent, and, with his sister, the haughty, stubborn high priestess of the volcano, entered the church.

In 1837 the great interest became general throughout all the islands. Fifteen thousand people, scattered up and down the coast for a hundred miles, could not be reached by one man ; and so whole villages gathered from miles away, and made their homes near the mission-house.

Hilo was crowded with strangers. Little cabins studded the place like the camps of an army, and the population increased to 10,000 souls. The old church was packed with a sweltering and restless mass of 6,000 souls. A new church near by took the overflow of 2,000, while hundreds pressed about the doors.

The revival was at its height Nov. 7, 1837. The crescent beach, dotted with native booths, reaching up into the charming groves behind, was in peaceful security. It was the hour of evening prayer. Suddenly a great cry and wail arose, and a scene of indescribable confusion followed. The sea, moved by an unseen hand, had suddenly risen, and the volcanic wave fell upon the shore like a· bolt from heaven. In a moment hundreds of people were struggling with the billows. "There was no sleep that night ; but the next day the meetings went on with renewed power, and through all the week, as the sea gave up one after another its dead, and the people bore them to their resting-places, the

Spirit sent home this new sorrow with divine effect."

No one knew his people better than Mr. Coan; but it was only by an exact system that he was able to care for his parish of 15,000 souls. His work was done by "drawing lines in the parish; by dividing the people into sections and classes; by attending to each class separately, systematically, and at a given time." Although thousands professed conversion during the years 1836–1837, only a small proportion of these had been received into the church. Over these converts Mr. Coan kept a vigilant watch; and, after a lapse of three, six, nine, or twelve months, selections were made for admission to the church.

The first Sunday of July, 1838, was a memorable one in the history of missions. On that afternoon 1,705 men, women, and children were baptized, and about 2,400 communicants sat down together at the table of the Lord, a scene that has had but one parallel since the day of Pentecost, and that was in connection with the labors of the Rev. Dr. Clough in India. In speaking of this scene, Mr. Coan said, " The memorable morning came arrayed in glory; the very heavens over us and the earth around us seemed to smile. From my roll each name was read ; and after all were seated, I passed back and forth between the lines, sprinkling each individual, until all were baptized." During the three years ending April, 1840, 7,382 persons were received into the church at Hilo. Between the years 1864 and 1868, six churches were built and set off from the old one, and each was under the care of a native preacher. Hawaiian money and labor have added many churches to this number ; and, in visiting the islands in 1870, Mr. Stoddard writes of these " pretty little meeting-houses, looking as though they had been baked in a lot, like a sheet of biscuits."

After an absence of more than thirty-five years, during which time Mr. Coan had baptized by his own hand 11,960 persons, at the invitation of the American

Board he returned, with Mrs. Coan, to the United States. The visit was full of interest; but the hoped-for restoration of health did not come to Mrs. Coan, and soon after their return to Hilo she died, Sept. 29, 1872.

Mrs. Coan's work was ever constant and tireless. She was a woman of high social and intellectual cultivation, and missionary work for her was a sacrifice. To her patient, unselfish, loving spirit was due a great part of her husband's success. While Mr. Coan was intent upon his great work as a missionary, he was not insensible to the scenes of natural beauty and grandeur about him. The scientific world is fortunate in having had upon the ground for nearly fifty years, when such volcanic forces were at play, one whose courage was equalled only by his graphic skill in portraying the most imposing of phenomena. One fruit of the faithful training of Mr. Coan is the growth of beneficence in the churches. More than $10,000 have come to the United States from the Hilo church.

This item adds strength to the statement of Lorrin A. Thurston, in a recent article in the *North American Review :* " The direct financial advantages accruing to the United States and its citizens, which they would *not* have received but for the treaty of 1876, have more than repaid, dollar for dollar, all loss by the United States through remission of duties under the reciprocity treaty."

Whence came this matter of political treaties and civilization to Hawaii? Surely through the American missionaries who first introduced Christianity and refined institutions to its people, prominent among whom was the Rev. Titus Coan, who, after a pastorate of forty-eight years, died at Hilo, Dec. 1, 1882.

III.

WILLIAM GOODELL,

Missionary to Turkey.

Born Feb. 14, 1792; Died Feb. 18, 1867.

III.

WILLIAM GOODELL.

It is many years since anything could be found that marked the birthplace of William Goodell in the little town of Templeton, Mass. But in 1792 there stood upon a hillside just outside the village, a one-story house, containing a garret floored with rough boards, beneath which were two rooms. One of these rooms answered the purpose of kitchen, dining-room, and parlor; the other was a small bedroom, containing a bed for the parents, and under this a trundle-bed that was rolled out at night for the children. The family library, composed of the Bible, Watts's " Psalms," Pike's " Cases of Conscience," the second volume of Foxe's " Book of Martyrs," and the " Assembly's Catechism," was counted the richest possession. 31

In this typical New England home was born William Goodell, Feb. 14, 1792. The piety of his father was of the rarest type; and he presents a vivid picture of the times, seated upon the stout old family horse, holding one child in his arms, his wife sitting on a pillion behind, with another child in her arms, and a third clinging to her — all on their way to the church in spite of storm or tempest.   Mrs. Goodell, the mother, though called to a life of pinching economy, and at length of painful and protracted illness, was the embodiment of delicacy, taste, and industry, as well as of meekness and devoted piety.

William Goodell had a delicate constitution, and it was evident early that he could not endure a life of manual labor.   His father earnestly desired that he should become a minister, and encouraged his son to attempt an education, although he had no money.   At length they heard of beneficiary aid given at Phillips Academy, and the son caught at this hope.   He walked and rode sixty miles to Andover, and walked the whole distance back home again, weary and footsore. The charity fund was overloaded; and he must, for one quarter at least, get on without help. The time soon came for the opening of the term, and without money or credit this lad set forth again; and there is no braver or more pathetic sight than that of William Goodell plodding his way through sixty miles, his trunk strapped to his back, to the permanent injury of his spine, the boys hooting at him in the streets. At Andover he found a temporary home in the house of an intemperate shoemaker, whose wife bestowed upon him with kindness the few comforts her very humble home provided. His family refer with pride to his first lesson at the academy. It was in the Latin grammar. When called on, he recited the first page *verbatim*, coarse print and fine, notes and all; then the second and third page in like manner, much to the satisfied amusement of his instructor, Mr. Adams; and from that moment he kept the good-will of his teachers.

At the close of this first quarter, Lieu-
tenant-Governor Phillips volunteered to
pay the boy's expenses. In his second
year his uncle, Solomon Goodell of Ver-
mont, wrote to Mr. Adams to know if the
boy was " worth raising," and received
such a reply that he sent him a fine yoke
of oxen. After his preparatory studies
he entered Dartmouth College, Sept. 24,
1813. Here, through the influence of Mr.
Adams, he received $100 per year from
the beneficiary funds of Kimball Union
Academy. This amount, together with
the money received from his teaching
school during the winter, defrayed his college expenses. The glimpses had of his
college life show the same mingling of
good-humor, earnest activity, and piety
which characterized his whole subsequent
life.

Near the close of his freshman year he
seems to have considered the question of
entering the missionary field; and in 1817
he became one of the sacred band in the
theological seminary at Andover, — the
missionary band.

After his graduation he made an engagement to visit several States, and awaken interest in foreign missions; and in this work met with much success. In September, 1822, the American Board held its annual meeting at New Haven, Conn.; and Mr. Goodell was then ordained, and destined to the mission in Palestine. On November 19 he was married to Miss Abigail Davis at Holden, Mass.; and a few days later Mr. and Mrs. Goodell embarked from New York in the vessel Shepherdess.

The Shepherdess, after a pleasant and prosperous voyage, arrived, Jan. 21, 1823, at the island of Malta, then a sort of schoolhouse where the missionaries bound for the Orient prepared for their future labors. There the Goodells remained until Oct. 22, 1823, when they left for Beyrout. Owing to the unsettled state of things at Jerusalem, it was deemed advisable to remain there for a time. Extracts from Mr. Goodell's letters give vivid pictures of their life and surroundings at this

place. A single passage will show how
many languages it was necessary the missionaries should be familiar with : "We
must daily read the Scriptures in ancient
Greek, modern Greek, Armenian, Arabic,
Italian, and English, and frequently hear
them read in Syriac, Hebrew, and French."

For a time everything connected with
the missionary work in Beyrout went on
prosperously. Within the first year an
order from the Maronite patriarch forbade
the people to receive the Holy Scriptures
circulated by the missionaries, and required all to return them or burn those
they had received. The war between
Greece and Turkey was then raging. The
lives of the missionaries were in constant
danger. For two years Mr. Goodell seldom closed his eyes to sleep without first
planning means of escape. His family
was at length sent to the mountains for
safety, and he could only visit them by
stealth. The continuance of the troubles
determined them to withdraw for a time
to Malta, where Mr. Goodell commenced

his great work of translating the Bible into
Armeno-Turkish; and here he issued the
entire New Testament.

In 1831 the Board sent Mr. Goodell to
the chief scene of his lifelong labors in
Constantinople. His wife and the women
who accompanied her were supposed to
be the first American women who ever
visited the place.

Two months after their arrival came
that terrible conflagration which swept
more than a square mile of the city with
indiscriminate destruction. It consumed
nearly all of Mr. Goodell's property, including manuscripts and books. For a
time he was a wanderer; and three weeks
later found himself in the vicinity of the
plague and cholera, with his wife and new-
born son. In spite of all his misfortunes,
he preached wherever he could find an
audience; and an American traveller who
was present at one of these services wrote:
" It is certainly not among the least of
the novelties of our situation to hear a
Yankee clergyman preaching in Italian

on the banks of the Bosporus, to an audience composed of representatives of half
a dozen nations assembled from various
quarters of the globe."

Within a few weeks Mr. Goodell had
established among the Greeks four so-
called Lancasterian schools, which were
soon largely increased in number. He
was also engaged in personal work with
the Armenians.

The first school for girls, in May, 1832,
created a great commotion. The gospel
began to take effect; and, in spite of many
trials, Mr. Goodell's work was most successful until the persecution, attended with
exile and imprisonment of converts, in
1839. At this time from six to ten thousand victims weekly were dying from the
plague. Everything was suspended but
sickness and death. The persecution did
not abate with the cholera; it grew fiercer
and fiercer, and threatened to break up all
missionary operations. But at the darkest
moment the sultan's army was defeated at
Aleppo; and in the sudden death of Sul-

tan Mahmoûd himself the hand of violence
was arrested.

In the year 1841 Mr. Goodell had accomplished what may be considered his
greatest achievement, — the translation of
the entire Bible into the Armeno-Turkish
language. It was a toilsome but loving
labor of many years, and was revised
again and again, to become one of the
landmarks of missionary effort in Turkey.
After the publication of the Armeno-Turkish Bible, he was enabled to engage in
a greater variety of labors, and to exert
a steadily growing influence within and
without the missionary circle.

To follow him through the details of
his missionary life and experiences, would
be to give a history of the mission in Constantinople for a generation. He preached
the gospel in six different languages, and
by his scholarship he achieved " a work
that fairly places his name beside that of
Wycliffe and Tyndale."

When Mr. Goodell entered Constantinople he was surrounded by misrepresen-

tation and opposition on every hand, and
his work seemed to promise little success ;
but he lived to rejoice in the achievement
of his fondest hope, to see the Turkish
government steadily change its attitude, a
formal bill of rights issued in 1839, a charter granted in 1850 for the Protestant
church, schools for girls, colleges and theological seminaries flourishing in the Turkish empire, an energetic band of churches
organized, and the American mission-work
in Turkey profoundly respected.

Mr. Goodell was himself deeply loved
and honored. After nearly thirty years
of voluntary exile, he and Mrs. Goodell
visited America in 1851, by special request
of the American Board. And for the two
years following he gave his time entirely
to travelling in this country in aid of foreign missions. He addressed more than
four hundred congregations, and met the
students of many colleges and theological
seminaries.

In 1853 Dr. and Mrs. Goodell returned
to Constantinople. In this year began the

Crimean War, which for a time clouded the missions in Turkey, and was the occasion of much anxiety to the friends of the cause throughout the world. But in 1856 the sacred edict, known as the Hatti-Humayoûn, was issued by the sultan, and was regarded by the friends of evangelical Christianity as a real charter of religious freedom to all subjects.

From this time Dr. Goodell continued his work with increasing influence and honor, and to the ever-enduring cause of Christianity. But at last failing strength and advancing years admonished him that his work in foreign lands was nearly done. He published forty-eight of his sermons in the Turkish language, wrote a farewell letter to the Protestant churches, and requested of the American Board a release.

After his arrival in America he made his home with his son in Philadelphia. Here he had a Bible-class of business men, and entered into the Christian activities of the times. During the remaining eighteen months of his life he visited many cities, and addressed large audiences. The most memorable of all his appearances in public was when he attended the meeting of the American Board in Chicago, October, 1865. No one will ever forget him who saw him there, with his velvet cap wrought with Arabic sentences by the schoolgirls of Aleppo, or who felt the hush when he rose and addressed the great assembly : "When I went from my native land in 1822 it was to go to Jerusalem; there I expected to live, to labor, and to die. I have never been there. I have now set my face toward the New Jerusalem, taking Chicago in my way."

Mr. Goodell died the following year; and Mrs. Goodell, the loving and faithful companion of his entire missionary life, who had shared his toils and trials by land and sea, who had lived to return with him to their native land, survived him but a short time, dying at the house of her son, Dr. William Goodell, in the summer of 1871.

IV.

WILLIAM CAREY,

Missionary to India.

BORN AUG. 17, 1761; DIED JUNE 9, 1834.

IV.

WILLIAM CAREY, " the father and founder of modern missions," was born at Paulersbury, Northamptonshire, Eng., Aug. 17, 1761. It is believed that his early ancestors were of considerable social prominence; yet at the time of his birth his father, Edmund Carey, was a journeyman weaver with a moderate income; but in 1767 he obtained the twofold office of schoolmaster and parish clerk.

William was taught by his father, and soon began an eager pursuit for knowledge, books of science, history, and travel being of especial interest to him. When very young he had great fondness for botany, and many were the specimens he brought home as a result of quests amongst the lanes and haunts of Whittlebury Forests. Physical ailments unfitted him for outdoor occupations; and at the age of seventeen he was apprenticed to a shoemaker, and thus linked, says Dr. George Smith, to a succession of scholars and divines, poets and critics, reformers and philanthropists, who have used the shoemaker's life to become illustrious.

A revolution took place in William Carey's life at his eighteenth year. Though brought up as a strict Churchman, as became the son of the parish clerk, he had fallen, through association with dissolute companions, into error; but owing to the efforts of a fellow-workman, he became converted, and from this time to the close of his life he was a devout student of the Scriptures. On June 10, 1781, he married Dorothy Plackett, his employer's sister-in-law. Mrs. Carey had little sympathy with her husband's tastes, but he always treated her with noble tenderness. Domestic and business troubles followed him closely. In her second year his little girl was taken from him; he himself was stricken with fever; starvation was staring him in the face, when his brother, only a youth, came to his relief, and, with the aid of friends, secured for him a little cottage in Pidding-ton, where Carey, besides continuing his shoemaking, opened an evening school. Attending the meetings of the association at Olney, Carey met the future secretary of the missionary society, Andrew Fuller. As a result of this meeting, Carey began to exercise his gifts as a preacher. The Dissenters in his native village soon sent for him to preach for them. His mother went openly to hear him, and declared if he lived he would become a great preacher; his father, being the parish clerk, heard him clandestinely on one occasion, and, though a reserved man, expressed himself as highly gratified.

Soon after Carey united with the church at Olney, and was by that body formally set apart for the work of the ministry. A field of action soon offered in Moulton, where he, after many preliminaries, was ordained pastor of the Baptist church.

Here his income was only ten pounds per annum; and after failing to increase it by teaching, he resumed his shoemaking in connection with the ministry. During the time of his pastorate in Moulton, Mr. Carey brooded continually over the condition of the world, and became convinced that the spreading of Christianity was a responsibility which all the converted ought to assume.

In April, 1789, Carey was called to the pastorate of Harvey Lane Church at Leicester. Here he was brought into association with men of culture, and books were freely placed at his disposal. The course of events was now rapidly moving toward the formation of the missionary society. At the annual meeting of the association held at Nottingham, Carey was one of the preachers. He chose for his text Isa. liv. 2, 3, which was paraphrased as follows: "Expect great things from God," "Attempt great things for God." The impression made by the discourse was so decided that the following resolution was passed:

" That against the next meeting at Kettering, a plan should be prepared for the purpose of forming a society for propagating the gospel among the heathen."

The meeting was duly held on October 2, and a collection of thirteen pounds made ; so the great missionary enterprise was duly inaugurated. At this time a ship surgeon, John Thomas, who had been in India, and had preached to the Hindus, had just returned to England, and was trying to establish a fund in London for a mission to Bengal. Carey suggested that it might be desirable for the society to co-operate, and a resolution was passed to send Mr. Thomas and Mr. Carey into India as missionaries. Many difficulties arose before their final departure, June 13, 1793, when Mr. and Mrs. Thomas and their child, Mr. Carey and his family, consisting of wife and three children, embarked. After a voyage of five months they arrived at Calcutta, November 9.

Thomas's knowledge of India was an advantage to Carey ; but his lack of judg-

ment, and the debts he had incurred in his
residence there, estranged from the missionaries some European Christians who
had otherwise been their friends. Calcutta
being found too expensive as a place of
residence, they removed to Bandel for a
time. But no facilities for missionary work
were afforded them there ; so they returned
to Calcutta, where they underwent vicissi-
tudes of all kinds until June, 1794, when
Mr. George Udny, at Malda (a former
friend of Mr. Thomas), offered the management of two indigo manufactories re-
spectively to Carey and Thomas. The
factory which Carey was to superintend
was at Mudnabatty ; and besides a salary
of 200 rupees per month, he was promised
a commission upon the sales. Carey at
once communicated with the secretary of
the society that he should not need more
supplies, and expressed the hope that another mission be begun elsewhere. The
duties at the factory allowed time for the
work of the mission.

Mr. Carey made such progress in the

study of Bengalee as to be able to preach intelligibly to the natives. He started a school, and worked vigorously at translation. In the midst of his great work he lost his little son Peter, and finally was himself prostrated with the fever, which lasted several months. Carey remained in Mudnabatty until Jan. 10, 1800, when, with his wife and four children, he joined a little colony of missionaries, who, through his influence, had come to India and settled at Serampore, a little village founded by the Dutch in 1755.

The missionaries found a home in a large house in the middle of the town, purchased from a nephew of the Danish governor. They lived in perfect unity, " and what one had was another's," and thus began the great missionary enterprise at Serampore. The name of the first Hindu convert was Krishnu Pal, and the baptism of this native was a most memorable scene. Carey going down into the river, taking first his son Felix and baptizing him, using English words; then Krishnu went down and was baptized, the words being in Bengalee. All was silence and attention. The governor could not restrain his tears, and every one seemed to be impressed with the solemnity of this sacred ordinance.

Feb. 7, 1801, saw the issuing of Carey's translation of the New Testament. On the completion of this great undertaking, a special meeting was convened for the purpose of giving thanks unto God. The publication of the Bengalee New Testament naturally directed attention to Mr. Carey. The eminent scholarship it disclosed pointed him out at once as the teacher who might fittingly occupy the Bengalee chair in the government college at Fort William. His first position was that of teacher of Bengalee, afterwards of Sanscrit and of Mahratta, with a salary of £600 per annum.

From teacher he became professor. As professor of the three Oriental languages his emoluments rose to £15,000. But the whole of this income, with the exception of some £40 needed for the support of

his family, he devoted to the interests of
the mission.   Carey held his position
of professor until 1830, within four years
of his death, and proved himself more than
equal to his office, winning the esteem and
affection of students and colleagues alike.
It was not to be expected that the Serampore labors would be allowed to proceed
without political interference.   Serious difficulties arose, threatening not only the
existence of the press, but of the mission
itself.   As the time drew near for the re-
newal of the East India Company's charter, the friends of missions directed their
efforts toward securing the introduction
of clauses permitting the free entrance of
missionaries into India, and liberty to
propagate the Christian religion.   The bill
passed the Commons, July 13, and was
accepted by the Lords, and entrance was
granted.

The new chapel at Calcutta was duly
opened, Jan. 1, 1809, and Carey conducted
the week-day services there.   And while his
professional engagements and his literary

pursuits detained him often in Serampore and Calcutta, yet he eagerly seized any opportunity that arose for itinerating, with a view to extending Christianity. In 1807 Mrs. Carey died, having long suffered from insanity; and in the following year Carey married Miss Charlotte Rumohr, of noble Danish descent. She entered heartily into all the concerns of the mission, and was a great help to her husband until her death, which occurred in 1820.

Besides translating the Bible into seven different languages, Mr. Carey wrote grammars and elementary books of all the languages he had acquired. The improvement upon native paper for press purposes, by manufacturing it so as to be proof against destruction by insects, was an immense advantage gained by the ingenuity of the missionaries, and the importation of a steam-engine of twelve horse-power for working their paper-mill was a striking evidence of the enterprise of these men.

No memoir of William Carey would be complete which did not record his benevo-

lent endeavors to improve the social condition of the natives of India. The first
reform he helped to effect was the prohibi-
tion of the sacrifice of children at the great
annual festival at Gunga Sangor. Another
reform to which Carey gave his determined
attention was the abolition of burning wid-
ows on the pile of their dead husbands.

The benevolent institutions for instructing the children of indigent parents origi-
nated in the philanthropic sympathies of
Carey; and in the year 1817 no less than
forty-five schools had been established. A
leper hospital was founded, and a vernacu-
lar newspaper published.

Carey possessed in not a few branches
of natural history a knowledge so scientific
that it was more than sufficient to command respect. His practical knowledge
of botany and agriculture resulted in very
material benefit to India, and lays that
country under a debt of obligation which
can never be discharged. In 1817 was
begun the missionary training institute,
which afterwards grew to a college, and

was placed upon the same basis as other colleges of Europe.

For forty-one years William Carey was spared to labor for the good of India. He outlived nearly all who were associated with him in his prolonged residence, unbroken by any return to England. He died June 9, 1834.

During his lifetime Carey's great attainments called forth honorable recognition. Brown University in the United States conferred upon him the degree of D.D. The Linnæan, Horticultural, and Geological Societies admitted him to their memberships; and men of high position, such as the Marquis of Wellesley and Lord Hastings, extolled his worth. But he cared little for worldly praise; his great desire "to be useful in laying the foundation of the Church of Christ in India" was surely accomplished, and he wished for "no greater reward," "no higher honor."

V.

WILLIAM G. SCHAUFFLER.

BORN AUG. 22, 1798; DIED JANUARY, 1883.

V.

WILLIAM G. SCHAUFFLER.

WILLIAM G. SCHAUFFLER was born at
Stuttgart, the capital of Würtemberg, Aug.
22, 1798. In consequence of the constant
wars which had shaken Europe ever since
the great French Revolution of 1789, the
fortunes of the Schauffler family became
depleted; and in 1804 William Schauffler's
father, Philip Frederick Schauffler, led a
band of colonists to Russia, where great
inducements were held out to German settlers by Catharine the Second, who desired
to people the uninhabited, though fertile,
lands of the Volga and Ukraina. These
colonists were exempted from all taxation
for thirty years; their descendants, now
very numerous, still inhabit the country
and preserve unbroken the German language and customs, and from them come

many of the emigrants now found in the
Dakotas and other parts of the United
States.

The Schaufflers, after being on the road
nine months, arrived in 1805 at Odessa,
then a village on the sea-coast of South
Russia, and governed by the Duke of
Richelieu, afterward premier under Louis
XVIII. of France. The governor knew
German well, and through his influence
Philip Schauffler was made mayor of the
German population of Odessa.

There were then no German schools in
the village, and the Schauffler children
were taught by a clerk of their father's.
William studied French with his sister, and
learned to play on the flute. He constructed a beautiful instrument, and all
his life charmed his friends by his exquisite playing. The Schaufflers were models
of morality, and entertained " orthodox "
views, but enjoyed few religious advantages. They, as a family, possessed an
innate refinement and culture ; and the
musical ability of the children caused their

entrée into circles far above them in social standing, and prevented their mingling with the uneducated, and for the most part unprincipled, Germans then inhabiting the village.

William learned a trade, and helped in the support of the family. Until " twenty-two years of age he lived in the world and for the world." Though given to much serious thinking, he became very fond of worldly amusements ; but his chief passion was music. In 1820 there came to Odessa the Catholic priest Lindl, afterward excommunicated from the Roman Church. He preached with great power, and drew young Schauffler to his services, where he was converted. Missionary work early attracted Schauffler's attention ; and five years later, at the age of twenty-seven, invited by " the ardent but eccentric Dr. Wolff," he left home and accompanied him to Persia. He barely escaped shipwreck before reaching the Bosporus.

He found the plans of Dr. Wolff impracticable, and now turned to Andover, Mass., instead of England, as he first intended, for preparation for a missionary career. After a weary voyage of four months, he arrived in Boston with eleven dollars in his pocket. He was cautiously, but politely, received by Secretary Evarts of the American Board, and by him advised to confer with the professors at Andover. His linguistic attainments won favor with them, and a year of preparation for the seminary was soon decided upon. He proposed to sell his flute to buy books, and to work at his trade for self-support. The students bought his flute for $50, then gave it to him on condition that he would play at their meetings.

He remained in Andover five years, engaging in arduous study and assisting the professors. Besides Greek and Hebrew, he studied Chaldee, Syriac, Arabic, Samaritan, Rabbinic, Persian, Turkish, and Spanish; but to accomplish this he abstained from all miscellaneous reading and hardly looked at a newspaper. He was entirely ignorant of the French Revolution

of 1830, and reached France in 1831 not
knowing Louis Philippe was on the throne.
While engaged in his scholastic course,
William often went to Lowell, Mass., then
just starting as a manufacturing centre, to
conduct religious meetings, and gave much
energy and zeal to this work.

He was ordained in Park-street Church,
Boston, Nov. 14, 1831, a missionary of
the American Board. He was first sent
to Paris to continue his linguistic studies,
but in a few months passed from the then
plague-smitten city to Odessa, by way of
his birthplace, and after a brief sojourn full
of evangelistic labor went on to Constantinople. He was sent to Smyrna to look
after mission interests, and here met and
soon became engaged to Miss Mary Rey-
nolds of New Haven, Conn., then teaching a mission-school. They were married,
Feb. 26, 1834, by Dr. Goodell, at the residence of Commodore Porter, the American
ambassador. In a little repast enjoyed at
their own room the evening after the cere-
mony, roasted potatoes and butter formed

the rarest viands, never having been introduced into Constantinople until Mr. Shauffler had them sent from Odessa.

The early part of the Schaufflers' married life was sorely tried by living in a plague-infested city, and by privations and sickness; but Mr. Schauffler in the midst of all labored earnestly in his translation of the Scriptures into Hebrew-Spanish, and preached on Sundays in English and German to local residents. In April, 1836, he took his family to Odessa, and here a second son was born to them, and here both children died; but in spite of this affliction he worked on, and many conversions took place during his sojourn.

In March, 1837, he and his wife returned to Constantinople; and while living here with Missionary Dwight's family, Mrs. Schauffler was exposed to the plague in caring for Mrs. Dwight, who died of it. Indeed, exposure to this terrible disease was an every-day occurrence to the Schaufflers; but their faithful care for the physical and spiritual needs of those about them can be appreciated only by those who witnessed their great work.

In September, 1839, the Schaufflers, with their infant son Henry, went to Vienna by way of South Russia, where crowds flocked to hear the preaching, though they had to walk long distances after their day's work, and sleep in wagons, stables, and other available places. In Vienna Mr. Schauffler held services during three winters in his own dwelling, attended by many Catholics, who joyfully received the news of a free salvation. The love, zeal, and faithfulness of the converts were most touching. Such were the people that papal Austria soon after put under the harrow of persecution. A fourth son was born to the Schaufflers in September, 1839. At this time Mr. Clay was the American ambassador; and the Schaufflers made many notable acquaintances, among them being the Archduchess Maria Dorothea, who became their friend.

William Schauffler was permitted, in a private interview, to lay before the em-

peror himself his printed Bible, upon
which he had lavished the great work of
his scholarship, and of which he had said,
"If I but live to finish this work, I shall
consider my missionary life a success,
secured and safe." The Bible was printed
in Vienna, because the best font of Hebrew type was found there. The verdict
of the Jews was entirely in its favor, and
the book went forth with the approval of
the rabbis. A larger edition followed a
few years later.

In July, 1842, the Schaufflers were back
at their station, and the Goodells entertained them until their own home was
ready for use. The Armenian persecution
was going on; and being a missionary to
the Jews, and having German servants, the
Schauffler home was the place of meeting
of the persecuted Armenian "Bible-read-
ers," and many and arduous were the cares
during this time. Mr. Schauffler had now
numbered ten years of missionary life, and
thus far he was sole representative of the
Jewish Mission from the United States;

and his chief co-operation seems to have
come from the English and Scotch, also
represented in the field, and afterwards
leading in the work, for the reason that
missions to the Jews never took a deep
hold upon the American Board.

At the meeting of the station in 1855,
it was recommended to the Board that
the Jewish Mission be relinquished to the
Scotch Free Church. It is not surprising
that after twenty-three years of service,
not the least of which was the work in
Salonica, Mr. Schauffler felt aggrieved at
this summary disposal of the mission. He
might have called for a reconsideration ;
but he did not care to do so, and refused
a position in the ranks of the Scotch brethren, and also declined an invitation to
enter the Armenian field. He had put
through the press a Hebrew grammar, a
Hebrew-Spanish lexicon of the Bible, and
a third popular translation of the psalms
into Spanish. He seemed to feel that his
work was done.

But at this time the mission appointed

Mr. Schauffler to present to the Evangelical Alliance, then meeting at Paris, the great question of religious liberty in Turkey, including the Mohammedans. The chief object was to induce the Alliance to plead with the sovereigns of Europe to use their influence with the Turkish sultan to abolish the death penalty among the Moslem converts to Christianity. The French members especially were reluctant to lay the case before Napoleon III. ; but by declaring that the little band of missionaries at Constantinople would fight the battle at any cost, and without the aid of their brethren if necessary, Mr. Schauffler carried the assembly. He had long before won the favor of the English ambassador, Sir Stratford Canning. The news of Sevastopol's fall was posted along the streets the very morning Mr. Schauffler left Paris, and at Stuttgart he was invited to speak on the Crimean War.

Having returned to Constantinople in February, 1856, he decided to enter the Islam field, and with his usual energy proceeded to acquire the Turkish tongue ; and through his activity a new mission was opened for the Turks, in the interest of which Mr. Schauffler visited this country a little later ; and after an absence of thirty-one years both he and his wife found a cordial welcome. To institute a new mission for the Turks on the very field of the Armenian mission, where race prejudices were antagonistic, and might call for separate buildings, Mr. Schauffler foresaw would prove too costly for the Board ; but he was encouraged to go forward, and, with some misgivings, after a time he resumed his work. The arduous task of translating the Scriptures into Turkish was before him. But difficulties soon arose, among them the entrance of the Propagation Society of England, and the determination in Boston not to institute a separate Turkish mission, but to have the Armenian mission cover the field ; and serious complications occurred, which resulted in Mr. Schauffler's resignation from the American Board. Thus summarily closed the " separate "

Turkish mission, as had the Jewish before it; but through all these trying times Mr. Schauffler's faith and charity prevailed, and his chief concern was for the diffusion of Christianity. His remaining years were given to his great work of Bible translation.

In 1874 the veteran missionary and his faithful helpmeet left Constantinople; and many a tear flowed, and many a benediction followed, from the home that had been theirs for forty years. After sojourning with their son Henry, a missionary of the American Board in Moravia, they came to New York to pass the rest of their days with their two younger sons. In January, 1883, Mr. Schauffler died; and his widow followed him in January, 1895.

His was a character singularly unselfish and pure. His rare scholarship, and especially his translation of the Bible into Osmanli-Turkish, procured for him from the University of Halle and Wittenberg the degree of Doctor of Divinity, and from Princeton College the degree of Doctor of

Laws. Nature endowed William Schauffler with a vigorous body, a character simple, honest, and grand, a generous, enthusiastic heart, and a symmetrical and
highly gifted mind, while grace developed
both heart and mind; and the obscure
young mechanic of Odessa became the
widely known, honored, and ardently loved
missionary, whose work will be for all
time.

VI.

GRIFFITH JOHN.

BORN DECEMBER 14, 1831.

VI.

GRIFFITH JOHN.

FOR many years the church of Christ had prayed that its missionaries might be admitted into China, and when the opportunity arrived, promptly sent forth its messengers of salvation into the crowded cities.

Conspicuous among these pioneers was Griffith John, born at Swansea, Wales, Dec. 14, 1831. His parents were religious and comfortably situated. His mother died of cholera in 1832. At eight years of age he was admitted a member of the church at Ebenezer, Swansea. At fourteen Griffith John began to preach the gospel, and from the first gave evidence of possessing oratorical gifts of the highest order. It was determined that a course of study would be of great benefit to him; and his father asked the Rev. E. Jacob, the pastor at Swansea, if " he would teach John a little." The kind-hearted pastor gratuitously taught him; and Mr. John resided with him from Nov. 13, 1848, until September, 1850.

In 1849 his father died; and from that time Mr. Jacob became a father to him, and was most assiduous in preparing his young charge for the career of great usefulness which he felt lay before him. In answer to the questions of the college authorities at Brecon when Mr. John was seeking admission, Mr. Jacob wrote: " Considering his age, he is decidedly the nearest to being a perfect or complete Christian of any I ever knew; his voice is sweet, his delivery easy, his preaching of extraordinary character." Mr. John entered college with the hope of becoming a successful and popular minister, but soon earthly ambition gave way to an ardent desire for missionary work among the heathen.

He was offered the pastorate of one of the most important Congregational churches; but he refused the invitation, and was accepted by the London Missionary Society. His first desire was to go to Madagascar, but he offered no objection when asked to go to China. Before leaving England, Mr. John married Miss Margaret Jane Griffiths, daughter of the Rev. David Griffiths of Madagascar. A more happy union could not have been made, and Mrs. John was a successful worker among the women in China. On the 21st of May, 1855, the Rev. Griffith John and Mrs. John sailed for Shanghai, arriving there Sept. 24, after a pleasant and uneventful voyage of one hundred and twenty days. At the time of Mr. John's arrival, the country was practically free for travellers with peaceful objects in view.

Mr. John entered upon his work with characteristic ardor. He studied hard during the voyage, and now applied himself to the acquisition of the language, with the

hope that in six months he might be able
to preach. In January, 1856, Mr. John
writes: "For some months I have been
in the habit of going into the temples, the
tea-gardens, and other places, to distribute
tracts and to preach as I could; now I am
able to speak for a half-hour at a time, and
to my great satisfaction, I find I am very
well understood." In speaking the Chinese language, much depends on the tones
and mere rising and falling of the voice.
This makes the acquisition of the spoken
language a tedious and difficult task.
Still more perplexing is the written language.

At first Mr. John accompanied other
missionaries in various preaching journeys; but in October, 1846, he started
upon an expedition, taking only Wong
the colporteur as assistant. They first
visited Swong Kong; they anchored for
the night four miles below the city, and
in the morning entered the west gate.
It was the time for the annual examination; and the candidates for literary honors

crowded the streets, affording intelligent audiences wherever the missionary and his helper chose to work. They had a good supply of books, which were eagerly sought after. The next day was the Lord's Day, but there is no Sabbath in China. All is noise, bustle, tumult, and impiety; but Mr. John returned to the boat, gathered the boatmen around him, and read prayers.

In October, 1857, Mr. John and the Rev. J. Edkins visited Soochow, which is regarded by the Chinese as one of their richest and most beautiful cities. They say to be happy on earth one must be born at Soochow, live in Canton, and die in Soochow; for in the first are the handsomest people, in the second the richest luxuries, and in the third the best coffins. Mr. John now devoted himself almost exclusively to itinerating, and visited a large number of towns and cities. In October, 1858, Mr. John and three of his brother missionaries resolved to make an extended tour, preaching and distributing books in all the cities along the Grand Canal as far as its

entrance into the Yellow River. They also
were anxious to ascertain what influence
the treaty of Tientsin between China and
England had had upon the people, and
how far mission-work could be carried on.
The Grand Canal is six hundred and fifty
miles in length, and is divided into three
parts, which were made under three different dynasties. By it and the rivers it
connects, there is an almost uninterrupted
water-way from the north to the south of
the empire.

Mr. John proceeded as far as he had
passports, and preached the gospel under
trials of all kinds in all towns that he was
able to enter. Revolution is the only
means the Chinaman has of getting rid of
bad governments; and it is associated in his
mind with patriotic deeds of heroism, and
with some of the brightest periods of his
national history. Between the years 1830
and 1840, an unusual number of rebellions,
inundations, and famines had caused great
discontent among the people. Thus the
country was very unsettled when Hung-

sewtsuen, the Taiping chief, arose. He was a poor lad, but possessed an able mind, and was essentially Chinese in his way of thinking; desiring notoriety, he resorted to unofficial ways, and in 1837 he had trances, and proclaimed himself a heavenly prince. In 1843 he began to study Christian tracts, and in 1847 put himself under the instruction of Mr. J. Roberts, an American missionary in Canton. His writings do not show that he appreciated the real spirit of Christianity, but the skill with which he turned some of its doctrines to his own use was really wonderful.

In 1851 Hungsewtsuen commenced his march through China, establishing himself, in 1853, in Nanking, which city he held until 1864. The missionaries resident in Shanghai were desirous of ascertaining the exact state of affairs among the Taipings, and Mr. John with five others visited Soo-chow and passed through novel experiences; all of them were in danger of being killed in an affray between the villagers and the insurgents. The leaders of the rebels were acquainted with many Christian truths, and always addressed the missionaries as " our foreign brothers."

In 1860 Mr. John resolved to go boldly to Nanking, the seat of the Taiping government, and endeavor to obtain from Kan Wang an edict of religious toleration. The distance to Nanking was about two hundred and fifty miles, and the missionaries were treated with marked respect in all the towns through which they passed. The journey was a complete success; and the edict obtained gave permission to all missionaries, whether Protestant or Catholic, to live in the insurgents' territory and carry on mission-work. Although the Taipings fell into many grievous errors, the seeds of Christianity were doubtless in the hearts of the leaders. They did one good thing by creating a vacuum, not only in the temples, destroying the idols, but also in the hearts of the people. It was the work of the missionary to fill this void.

The new treaty between England and China opened the northern provinces to

direct mission-work, and the great network
of rivers and canals made many parts of
the vast empire easy of access. Hankow,
situated on the Yang-tsi, is accessible to
ocean steamers at all times of the year.
Mr. John had heard of, read about, and
many times longed to visit, this great em-
porium of China, and with Mr. Wilson
finally arrived there on the 21st of June,
1861. It was a most flourishing mart,
people from eighteen provinces meeting
there to exchange the varied products of
the great empire. Mr. John, with his characteristic promptitude, commenced preaching on the first day; and from that time
to the present, Hankow has had the gospel daily proclaimed by an ever-increasing
number of missionaries.

On the 12th of September Mr. John removed his wife and children to Hankow,
and worked with great energy, being aided
by two native assistants. His audiences
were very large. In August, 1861, Hien-
fung, the Emperor of China, died ; and the
change in the government was speedily felt

all over the empire. The people were more docile and susceptible to influences from without. The magistrates of Hankow were very friendly towards Mr. John, and he spoke on Christianity in the highest circles of society. Early in the year 1862 Mr. John reported steady progress. At the close of twelve months' labor the infant church at Hankow numbered twelve members.

Soon after his arrival at Hankow, Mr. John determined that Wuchang, being the provincial capital of Hupeh, would be a most desirable place for mission-work, and for four months labored steadfastly to obtain a foothold there. At the end of that time, and after a severe conflict with the authorities, literati, and gentry, he erected, upon purchased land, buildings costing £500, and consisting of a chapel-house, two schoolrooms, and hospital. And so with great judgment and foresight, Mr. John founded the Hankow Mission.

In 1864 Mrs. John, with her entire family of four children, was obliged to visit England for several months for a

climatic change. Mrs. John returned to
Hankow with her youngest child in 1865.
In 1867 Mr. John reported an increase
of fifty-one members to the church. The
great event of the year 1868 was the missionary journey of Mr. John and the late
Mr. Wylie of the British and Foreign Society to Chung-tu, the capital of Si-chuen,
and their return through the province of
Shen-si, a distance of three thousand
miles. Never before had the gospel been
so widely published in China by the voice
of a missionary. After his return Mr.
John writes, " I feel, in a way I have
never felt before, that the valley of the
Yang-tsi and the Hau have been taken
possession of in the name of Christ, and
that it is for me to live and die for the
millions of precious souls that line these
two magnificent streams." In 1869 Hankow and Wuchang were visited by a flood
which caused over a hundred thousand
people to flee to the hills near Hankow.

At this time Mr. John's family suffered
much from the cold, and their discomfort

was increased by small-pox among his children.   In spite of all he worked vigorously, often preaching four times a day and walking long distances. He was at this time rewarded in part, by having five converts coming forward and offering their services gratuitously as evangelists — a thing he had long desired.

Mr. John had for some time thought of visiting his native land, and in September, 1870, arrived with his family safely in London.   During the next three years he preached in England, and his eloquent appeals in behalf of China were most stimulating.   In 1872, at the directors' invitation, he preached the annual sermon at the anniversary of the London Missionary Society, which was afterwards published under the title of " Hope for China."

In 1873 both Mr. and Mrs. John were anxious to return to China ; they sailed from Liverpool Feb. 8.   It was a cold day, and Mrs. John never rallied from the effects of her exposure to the weather.   The heat of the Red Sea was most trying, and her suffering increased, and her gentle spirit fled just as the rising of the glorious Eastern sun lighted the vessel's way into the harbor of Singapore.

Mr. John arrived at Hankow in a very distressed condition, but plunged into his work again, although his feelings of loneliness and sorrow were intense. The church now numbered over two hundred members, and monthly additions were made. As Hankow is purely a business mart, very many who were converted and baptized returned home, often to distant provinces. Thus from the centre of the empire ran light and life to every province.

During the winter of 1873–74, a new and commodious hospital was erected at Hankow, at a cost of £1,350, subscribed by foreigners and natives. In 1859 Mr. John wrote a valuable paper on "The Ethics of the Chinese, with Special Reference to the Doctrines of Human Nature and Sin." In 1882 he wrote "A Plea for China," also "China, her Claims and Call," and a valuable booklet entitled, "Spiritual Power for

Missionary Work." It is chiefly through his literary efforts that Mr. John's name has become so well known in the Celestial Empire. In no country in the world are there so great inducements to the missionary to use the press as a means of making known the truth as in China. The number of readers among the people is very large. Every hamlet and village has its school. Everywhere education is held in highest esteem. The catalogue of the Central China Tract Society contains upwards of thirty books and tracts from Mr. John's pen, and every year over half a million of his publications are circulated throughout China.

In October, 1874, Mr. John married the widow of the Rev. Dr. Jenkins of the Methodist Episcopal Church of America; by her spiritual power and earnest work she was a great aid to her husband, and through her many converts were made among the Chinese women. Mrs. John was greatly interested in the sailors; and during the tea season of 1875, Mr. and

Mrs. John opened their house nightly to them, and ten conversions took place.

Early in May, 1878, Mr. John rendered great assistance to a mission sent out by the Established Church of Scotland, to be located at I-Chan, a city nearly four hundred miles up the river. In 1879 he was greatly cheered by the opening of a purely Chinese hospital in Hankow by one of the converts, Wang Kien-tang, who had been trained by Dr. Reid.

In 1880 Mrs. John on account of ill-health left Hankow for England, but was finally compelled to visit America. Here other symptoms developed, and Mr. John was summoned by cablegram to New York. He arrived there in March, 1881, and was received very kindly by Rev. Dr. Bevan. Mrs. John sustained a successful surgical operation, and in July, 1881, returned with her husband to England, where they spent the winter with their friends. They, however, longed for their loved toil, and sailed for Hankow in February, 1882.

In 1883 Mr. John saw with pleasure the completion of a building called The Sailors' Rest. Ever-widening success attended the mission of Hankow; but in the midst of it he experienced a sad loss in the death of his wife, who died on Christmas, 1885. Although Mr. John's life was clouded by sorrow and loneliness he worked on, and in 1886 saw the erection of a beautiful new chapel with large vestry, native pastor's house, girls' school and teachers' rooms. Like the Sailors' Rest, they were the outcome of that pilgrimage of pain made by Mrs. John to New York and England. On the morning of Sunday, June 27, four hundred and fifty Christians attended service in the new chapel; and the Rev. David Hill, Chairman of the Wesleyan Hankow Mission, preached from Gen. xxviii. 17, "This is none other but the house of God, and this is the gate of heaven."

This year, 1887, is memorable for the remarkable proclamation from the Tsung-li Yamen (government office) at Pekin, bidding the people in general live on terms of friendship and good-will with their Christian neighbors, and exhorting all local magistrates to treat Christian applicants for justice with perfect impartiality

The year 1888 found the Hankow Mission receiving monthly accessions in very encouraging numbers, and Mr. John worked steadily at his great task (now completed) of translating the Old Testament into " easy Wen-li."

In Mr. John, China has been favored with a highly efficient and indefatigable worker; and the earnest prayer of all who are acquainted with the great work he has done, is that he may long be spared to further advance the cause of Christ among the " black-haired race " by tongue and pen, and that through his example many may be influenced to follow in his footsteps, and devote their lives to this most noble enterprise.

VII.

ELIJAH COLEMAN BRIDGMAN.

Born, April 22, 1801; Died, November 2, 1861.

VII.

ELIJAH COLEMAN BRIDGMAN.

"The Puritan recognized God in his soul, and acted."

ELIJAH COLEMAN BRIDGMAN, imbued with the characteristics of his forefathers, was not a man of speculation, of creative ability, or of startling originality; but he was one who united within himself the chief elements of Puritanism, — faith and action. "He believed God; yes, actually believed him, and scattered broadcast the seeds of his belief." He was born at Belchertown, Mass., April 22, 1801; and the subtile moral atmosphere which then pervaded New England homes became a part of him.

His school-life began in his native town, was continued at Amherst, and completed at the Andover Theological school. As a boy, Mr. Bridgman was obedient and affectionate ; to his mother's influence he owed his early conversion. While still in college he conceived a desire to become a missionary; and his wish being in full accord with his family, he readily accepted, on his Class Day, an invitation offered by the American Board (aided by the liberality of Mr. R. M. Olyphant of New York) to go to China.

Mr. Olyphant made a contract with the Board to furnish passage and Mr. Bridgman's living expenses in China for a year.

Mr. Bridgman sailed from New York Oct. 14, 1829, and arrived at Macao, China, Jan. 22, 1830. He was warmly welcomed by Dr. and Mrs. Morrison.

Dr. Morrison went to China in 1807, under appointment of the London Missionary Society, and established the first Protestant Mission in that land.

Feb. 25 Mr. Bridgman arrived in Canton, and immediately established his residence in the American factories.

The foreign factories at this time were

thirteen in number, and built of brick or granite, and floating flags of different nations, presented to a stranger a picturesque and striking contrast with the native architecture of the " Celestial Empire."

Dr. Morrison held Sunday services in the American factory; and in his journal of March 1, 1830, Mr. Bridgman records the presence of twenty English-speaking residents.

Having received books and all necessary help from Dr. Morrison, Mr. Bridgman immediately began the study of the Chinese language, of which in later life he wrote, " There is no language so different from all others as the Chinese, and no other is acquired with so much difficulty by foreigners. In this point of view it has doubtless done infinitely more than ' the great wall ' to preserve the Chinese in their exclusiveness, hostile to international intercourse, and for many centuries almost hermetically sealed from the influences of Christianity."

Mr. Bridgman's first year in China was

given to study, to the teaching of English to several Chinese lads, and, in spite of the authorities' edict, to preaching the gospel whenever chance permitted. In May, 1832, at the suggestion of Dr. Morrison, he edited the *Chinese Repository*, a monthly magazine intended to arouse in the Christian world an interest in the spiritual awakening of China. This magazine was conducted by Mr. Bridgman until 1851 (after which time Dr. Williams became editor), and is now valuable as a reference-book.

In 1834, Aug. 1, Dr. Morrison, the veteran missionary, died. Of him Dr. Bridgman wrote, "In making known our holy religion to the Chinese, no one has done more." In October, 1834, Mr. Bridgman was called upon to preach the funeral sermon of Lord Napier, who had been sent out by the British government to protect the interests of English commerce at the port of Canton. After her return to England, Lady Napier wrote to Mr. Bridgman, "I have sent copies

of your sermon to all our own people;
and many a one amongst the lonely
valleys of Ettrick will bless your name
for the kindness you showed at all times
to our beloved dead."

In 1836 Mr. Bridgman began the translation of the Bible; but later the printing of the same was interrupted by the
" opium war." In March, 1839, trade
was suspended; the Chinese government
detained foreigners in Canton, and tumul-
tuous mobs were the order of the day.
In the midst of all, Mr. Bridgman was
not an idle spectator. In August, 1840,
he wrote : " The gauntlet has been thrown
down. After a friendly intercourse of
two hundred years, Great Britain finds
herself at war with the Chinese."

The war terminated in favor of the English, 1842 ; indemnity was granted, several
ports opened, and to the British government was ceded the city of Hong-Kong.
To this place Mr. Bridgman moved July 1,
1842 ; and here he prepared the " Chinese
Chrestomathy," a volume of seven hundred

and thirty pages. During this year the University of New York conferred upon Mr. Bridgman the degree of D.D.

In 1844 the United States of America sent the Hon. Caleb Cushing to the Chinese court; and July 3 a treaty of peace, amity, and commerce was concluded between the two nations, and foreigners were allowed residence at Canton, Amoy, Fuchau-fu, Ningpo, and Shanghai. By consent of the American Board, Dr. Bridgman and Dr. Peter Parker became secretaries to the legation; and of their services Mr. Cushing said officially and privately, " Their intimate knowledge of China and the Chinese made them invaluable as advisers, and their high character contributed to give weight and moral strength to the mission."

The year 1845 was made memorable in the history of missionary work by an edict from the Chinese emperor for the toleration of Christianity throughout the Empire.

The Chinese Repository of June, 1845, records the marriage of the Rev E. C.

Bridgman, D.D., with Miss Eliza Jane Gillett of New York.

Dr. and Mrs. Bridgman established a residence in Canton, where their work was supplemented and cheered by the co-operation of Dr. and Mrs. Parker.

The home of the Bridgmans was rented from a salt merchant, and partly built in foreign style. The first story was occupied by the coolies (servants), the second was the printing establishment, and the third afforded apartments for the family. And here in a small study-room sat Dr. Bridgman day after day, busy in his great work of translation, or patiently talking with the natives (from the Buddhist priest to the Chinese soldier) of the life of the Great Teacher. In the autumn of 1845 Mrs. Bridgman began the education of two Chinese girls; and these children formed the nucleus to a female school subsequently established under her care. Believing his first duty was to make known the truth, "to preach the gospel," Dr. Bridgman held daily services in Dr. Parker's ophthal-

mic hospital, and also preached to the multitude in the streets, holding always to the
desire for conversions first, and later for
baptism and churches.   In their attempts
to teach in neighboring vicinities, Dr.
and Mrs. Bridgman often exposed themselves to danger, and on one occasion
nearly sacrificed their lives to the infuri-
ated mobs.

Dr. Bridgman, being appointed by his
missionary brethren as delegate to the
committee assembled in Shanghai for the
revising of the Scriptures, established a
residence in that city, June 23, 1847; and
then, in addition to his labor of translation,
Dr. Bridgman assumed and carried on the
work of a clergyman, and gathered about
him a native church.   In 1850 he wrote
to the Secretary of the American Board :
" More than twenty years have now passed
since the first messengers from the churches
in America reached the land of Sinim.   In
these twenty years what changes have we
seen ! and now nearly a hundred laborers,
men and women, have *free* access to mil-

lions of people. The first fruits of a great
and glorious harvest begin to appear."

In 1852 Dr. Bridgman's health failed,
and with Mrs. Bridgman and a Chinese
pupil he returned to America for change
and a short visit. He arrived in New
York June 16 ; and then " railways, the
electric telegraph, and all the developments that two and twenty years had
produced, burst upon him with so much
interest, that it gave vigor to his frame,
and rejuvenated his whole being." The
four months of his visit were passed with
friends in the dear native State, and then
in journeying from place to place, to address assemblies in behalf of China. Returning, Dr. Bridgman and party visited
San Francisco, February, 1853, where Dr.
Bridgman took part in the dedicatory exercises of a church built for the Chinese.
A passage of thirty-eight days brought
the party safely to China. They arrived
at Shanghai, May 3 ; and on the 19th
Dr. Bridgman resumed his work of translation.

In September, 1854, Dr. Bridgman cordially welcomed Mr. Aitchison, and Mr. and Mrs. Blodget, who came to China under the appointment of the American Board. A mission was begun at Shanghai, a church formed, of which Dr. Bridgman was pastor until the time of his death. Dr. Bridgman was social in his instincts, ardent in friendships, and, interested in whatever could in any way conduce to the welfare of China, he was always ready to perform his part in every enterprise that aimed at that object. He was President of the Shanghai Literary and Scientific Society, and of the Morrison Educational Society; he was also officer and working-member of the North China branch of the Asiatic Society. He often entertained the plenipotentiaries of the four great treaty powers, — England, France, Russia, and the United States.

In the midst of active and unfinished labors, with his armor still about him, Dr. Bridgman died, Nov. 2, 1861. Thirty-two years of his life he gave to China, found-

ing in that land the first American mission, and leaving an impress upon his great
work which shall be forever indelible.

After her husband's death, Mrs. Bridgman returned to America; but her heart
was in China, and, although delicate in
health, " she went forth alone at fifty-nine
years of age to take up her work again.
To the mission at Peking she gave $12,500,
and established at that place a boarding-
school for girls. Four years later (1867)
she gave money and labor to founding a
girls' school in Shanghai; but her zeal
was here beyond her strength, and Nov.
10, 1871, she followed her husband to rest
in the city where most of their years together had been spent."

VIII.

BISHOP JAMES MILLS THOBURN.

Born, March 7, 1836.

VIII.

BISHOP JAMES MILLS THOBURN.

AMONG the many valuable gifts made by the Scotch-Irish stock to humanity in general, and Methodism in particular, Bishop Thoburn is not the least. His parents came to Ohio from the north of Ireland in 1825. He was born near St. Clairsville, Ohio, March 7, 1836. One incident of his childhood deserves record, as serving to show the nature of the influences thrown around him in his childhood. It is related by his sister, Miss Isabella Thoburn, who for the last twenty-five years has been at the head of a most useful girls' school in Lucknow, and was, indeed, the first missionary sent out by the Woman's Foreign Missionary Society of the M. E. Church. Writing of her father and mother, she says, "They bought a farm in Ohio, for which they could not make full payment, and were obliged to give a mortgage. It was when the harvest had been sold, and when the final payment was made, my father came home with two gold eagles above the amount of the debt. The announcement was made to the family; for every child had been made to feel that he shared the responsibility, and so was allowed to share the pleasure. Then father took out the two pieces of money, and said, 'We will give ten dollars to the Missionary Society for a thank-offering; and this,' he added, giving mother the other ten, ' is for your new cloak.' She held it thoughtfully a moment, and then, giving it back, said, ' Put this with the other piece for the thank-offering, and I will turn my old cloak.' " With such training it is not surprising that both brother and sister so promptly placed themselves on the missionary altar.

The father died in 1850; and James soon after left home, and practically began life for himself. Aided somewhat by his mother at the outset, he entered Allegheny College; but most of the funds for his college course he secured himself through teaching and other means. He graduated June 24, 1857. Two weeks later he began to preach in Stark County, Ohio. In March, 1858, he was admitted into the Pittsburg Conference, and sent as junior preacher to the Marlborough Circuit.

When he was only seventeen, he read one day a sermon of Dr. Olin's, in a little book called " Early Piety." As he perused a passage which called attention to the fact that it must be young men who should go forth as missionaries, " there flashed upon my mind and heart," he says, " a clear impression that my life-work would be in the missionary field." He was converted about eighteen months later, soon after he was nineteen ; and the conviction that God meant him to go abroad became still more deeply rooted. But he took up the work at home until the more definite call should come. It came in the latter part of 1858. The mission to India had been founded by

Dr. Wm. Butler the year before, and now search was being made for six young men to go to his help. When young Thoburn read the strong appeal to this end in the *Christian Advocate*, he was powerfully moved. God also manifested his approval, the widowed mother put no hindrance in the way, and the missionary authorities were glad to make the appointment. The final determination was reached by Jan. 1, 1859; and subsequent events have made it abundantly clear that no mistake was made.

He sailed from Salem, Mass., April 12, in a small ice-ship bound for Calcutta. The missionary party consisted of nine, — four men and their wives, besides Thoburn, who was the youngest of the company. Five of the nine have for many years been in the heavenly land; the other four, — Dr. and Mrs. Parker, and Dr. Waugh, with the Bishop, — are still at work in India. They landed at Calcutta, Aug. 21, 1859, and were warmly welcomed by Dr. Butler. Proceeding as speedily as possible to Lucknow, the forces were carefully distributed. Mr. Thoburn found himself assigned to Nynee Tal, in the mountain province of Kumaon.

He was now fairly launched on that life to which his thoughts had for so long a time been tending, and in which he was destined to make so notable a record. If he had the inexperience of youth, being only twenty-three, he had also its vigor and hopefulness, being, moreover, by nature of an especially buoyant and sanguine temperament. For four years Nynee Tal, beautiful for situation, was his home, if home a bachelor missionary can be said to have at all. Increasingly conscious of this great lack, he took to himself a wife, Dec. 16, 1861, marrying Mrs. Minerva R. Donney, whose husband, one of the party of nine, had died within a few weeks after reaching the country. He applied himself so diligently to the study of the language, that just a year after leaving St. Clairsville, and only about six months after reaching his station, he was able to preach with considerable freedom in the bazaar, and in a few months more he could conduct an entire service in the chapel; which is very unusual proficiency. In preaching, school-teaching, building, and holding services in English for the soldiers and other European residents of the station, the time passed quickly away. But, with the ignorance and enthusiasm of youth, too much was attempted, and a break-down in health was the result. A far heavier blow than this before long descended. In November, 1862, the gifted, devoted wife, on whose living so much seemed to depend, was translated, while the glow of the upper temple filled the lowly dwelling. "I am glad," she said, "that life has been given me, that I might have the privilege of dying." The baby boy thus sadly bereft was only four weeks old. In the following autumn the father, with his tender charge, got away for a greatly needed furlough, and reached his American home again during Christmas week of 1863.

While in America, tempting offers were

made him of employment at home; and
this, in conjunction with his weak state
of health and some other considerations,
came perilously near to wrecking his missionary career. He had actually concluded
to give up India; but on announcing his
determination to his sister Isabella, she reminded him of his call from God to the
work in India, and then said, —

"My advice is this: Whenever God
gives you an equally clear call to leave
India, you may safely give it up. Have
you any such call now?"

This pointed question extinguished the
false lights which had come so near to
leading him from the foreign field, and
all thoughts of abandoning India speedily
vanished.

He reached the seat of the India Conference at Moradabad, Feb. 1, 1866, and
was appointed to Paori, some five days'
journey west of Nynee Tal. Here he
labored two years, becoming much interested in the pilgrims who thronged the
mountain roads on their way to the fa-

mous Hindu shrines of Kedarnath and Badrinath, but not finding them favorable for missionary work. During the whole of the first year there was but one baptism. By the close of the second year the little church had six members and seven probationers. For the next two years, 1868 and 1869, Moradabad was his station; and in 1870, his sister having just arrived to begin the girls' school in Lucknow, he removed to that famous old capital. He was now presiding elder of the district, as well as charged with a variety of other functions; but his health was well established, and he greatly enjoyed the work.

Among the enterprises which here emanated from his fertile brain worthy of mention, is the *Lucknow Witness*, established April, 1871, and still flourishing at Calcutta, under the name of *The Indian Witness*. It had, almost from the first, a larger circulation than any other Christian religious paper in the Empire, and still maintains itself easily in the lead.

He soon developed also quite an extensive work among the English-speaking people of the city, who had been hitherto greatly neglected. And this received a great impetus by the coming of William Taylor, — now Bishop Taylor, — whose advent in Lucknow, Nov. 25, 1870, marked an important epoch. Revivals followed his preaching, not only there, but in all the chief cities of India; and the foundations of three new conferences were laid. It was mainly in connection with the work thus inaugurated that Dr. Thoburn's great success was to be achieved and his chief distinction reached.

In January, 1874, he was transferred by Bishop Harris to Calcutta, to follow up the work begun by William Taylor; and from this time he became the virtual head of the "Bombay and Bengal Mission," organized in 1876 as the South India Conference. A great church, costing eighty thousand rupees, and seating some sixteen hundred people, was soon built to accommodate the crowds that thronged to his preaching, and a continuous revival extended through every month of the year. Work was vigorously prosecuted among the sailors and among the Bengalis, and beginnings were made of what subsequently became two flourishing boarding-schools.

In June, 1879, in response to invitations to visit Rangoon, the capital of Burma, he went across the Bay of Bengal, and in two weeks' evangelistic services a Methodist church was initiated there which has since developed into a prosperous mission, with a multiplicity of successful departments. The same thing was done at the beginning of 1885 for Singapore. Dr. Thoburn went there with Mrs. Thoburn (he had married Nov. 11, 1880, Miss Anna Jones, M.D., of Kingston, Ohio) and Mr. Oldham. In a brief but most vigorous campaign of three weeks, a little church of seventeen members was organized, and matters put in such shape that the Malaysian Mission speedily got upon its feet. When it is remembered that in both of

these cases the missionary went forth with
no resources behind him, and no assurance
of help before him, except in the ever-sure
promises of God, it will be seen that an
achievement of no small moment was in-
volved. Dr. Thoburn has never hesitated,
with a hopefulness, courage, and faith worthy of all admiration and imitation, with
a trust in God, in himself, and in the
people rarely equalled, and with such a
measure of the divine indorsement in the
results reached as has silenced objections
or criticisms, to throw himself into the
breach whenever the cause of God seemed
to demand a forward movement. He has
developed, as the years have rolled on,
qualities of leadership of the most marked
character.

When the General Conference of 1888
arrived, Dr. Thoburn was unanimously
chosen by his brethren of Bengal to represent them, it being the strong expectation,
as well as desire, that he would be elected
to the new bishopric in India. This expectation was promptly and cordially grat-

ified. And Bishop Thoburn, as he has travelled throughout the Indian Empire during the past seven years, holding conferences, and directing the labors of his rapidly growing hosts, besides making frequent visits to America in the interests of his vast diocese, has abundantly justified the wisdom of the step taken at that time. In his report to the General Conference of 1892, the bishop was able to tell of four years' steady growth, during which the old North India Conference had more than quadrupled the large membership with which she entered upon the quadrennium, and the smaller conferences had doubled. He told of a membership of 30,000, a Christian community of 50,000 souls, and no less than 55,243 in the Sunday-schools. These large figures have all been marvellously increased since then, the membership having been more than doubled again, with other growth in proportion. Indeed, a work has broken out in the Methodist Mission of North India in the past six years, the like of which has probably never

before been anywhere seen. Some fifteen
or sixteen thousand Hindus have yearly
been baptized; and as many more are continually in waiting, whom the preachers
have to hold back, not being at all able
with any staff that can be employed to
overtake the task of properly instructing
this immense multitude. It is the harvest
from over thirty years of wisely planned
and energetically executed sowing. It is
mostly among the low castes; although all
classes, even the highest, are affected.
There seems at present no indication that
the work will stop, and no limit to it except
the ability of the toilers.

That the excellent generalship of the
bishop, his good judgment, noble example, and Christlike spirit, have been the
main factors in the success of the work, all
clearly see and willingly admit. He has
been a ceaseless inspiration and an unfail-
ing resource to the laborers. With an eye
on the entire field which he frequently
traverses, he strengthens each weak point
by prompt transfers of help, and dissemi-

nates the knowledge of the most approved methods. He has also raised by his personal exertions large sums of money, without which, time and again, the work must have been seriously crippled. Not yet threescore, although more than thirty-five years a missionary, it would seem that, by the blessing of God, he might be able for many years to come to lead on the conquering army of Christ in India to yet grander victories. He says that he hopes to live to lead an assault upon the gates of hell with a million Indian Christians at his back. It is surely not beyond the possibilities of Divine grace and power. May it become a living fact!

IX.

BISHOP SAMUEL ADJAI CROWTHER.

Missionary to Africa.

BORN 1808.   DIED DEC. 31, 1891.

IX.

BISHOP CROWTHER's youth was passed in
the shadows of Darkest Africa, and under
the spell of peculiar and depressing super-
stitions ; in the midst of wars, cruelty, and
bitter oppression. His home was in the
Yoruba country, one of the many states or
kingdoms into which Western Africa is divided. It lies to the west of the Niger
River, and forms a part of the slave coast
on the Gulf of Guinea, the country that
for so many years furnished the slaves
which supplied the markets of the world.

To supply this growing demand for
slaves, the country was kept in a continuous state of warfare, the chiefs contract-
ing to furnish the slaves, making raids
upon the neighboring tribes, and, it is
said, not infrequently swooping down upon
their own villages.

The usual plan was to make the attack in the night-time, set fire to the humble homes, and while the inhabitants were trying to escape, seize and bind them with heavy chains, fastened about the neck and wrists, killing all who offered resistance. The prisoners were then joined together, forming a long line, and driven with great cruelty from the smoking ruins of their homes. Thus in one night a large village would be completely destroyed. If any on the long march, under the load of galling chains, became unable to proceed, or an infant became troublesome, they were left to perish in the forest, or were killed on the spot.

Such were the experiences that came into the childhood of Bishop Crowther.

At the age of eleven years, in the year 1821, he was living with his father, mother, and three other children, in the flourishing village of Oshogun, containing over six thousand inhabitants, situated in Yoruba.

One morning very early, without the least warning, they were suddenly surrounded by an army of men-stealers, headed by Mohammedan Foulah. Men who attempted to resist were stricken down at their doors. Among these was the father of little Adjai, as he was then called. The mother with her children tried to escape into the bush; but they were pursued, lassoed, and brought back, chained, linked to others, and marched away.

In their long journey they passed other towns, where they saw some of their relatives who had met a like fate. After two days of tramping, goaded by the lash of the cruel slave-driver, they reached the place of the chief, where they were allotted to their future owners; Adjai and one of his sisters falling to the chief, while the mother and remaining children went to other persons.

Adjai was, however, soon sold from his sister, and, after passing through several hands, was finally landed on the coast, and put into the crowded slave-pen, or barracoon, where he was kept four months, to await the collection of a sufficient number to make up the ship's load. When this had been done, they were stowed away in the hold of the vessel, — a hundred and eighty-seven miserable creatures, — there to endure still greater sufferings than any that had yet fallen to them.

But suddenly there comes a change! A British man-of-war, sent out for this purpose, overtakes and captures the slave-ship, and liberates the slaves, who in their misery and despair cannot at once realize what has happened, and that they are now among friends. They mistook a pig hanging up, partly dressed, to be one of their number who had been slain; and the cannon-balls strewn around the deck they thought were negro heads.

They were taken to Liberia, and given to the care of the mission at Free Town. The boy Adjai was put into the mission-school, and was from the first a very apt scholar. After four years of instruction under the care of the Rev. Mr. and Mrs. Weeks, he became a Christian, and was

baptized at the age of fifteen, taking the
name of Samuel Adjai Crowther. He was
trained in manual labor, and became quite
proficient in the use of tools. In 1826 he
was taken to England by Mr. and Mrs.
Davey on a visit, spending part of the
time in a school at Islington, returning at
the end of a year to Sierra Leone. He
was one of the first half-dozen natives who
entered the Yourah Bay College. A few
years later he became an assistant teacher
in the college. With this mark of confidence shown by his friends, there came to
him the inspiration to devote his life and
all of his power to the uplifting of his own
people.

In a letter to a friend he writes : —

" From this period I must mark the unhappy but blessed day, which I shall never
forget in my life ; unhappy because it was
the day on which I was violently turned
out of my father's house and separated
from my relatives, and made to experience what it is to be in slavery ; blessed
because it was the day which Providence

had marked out for me to set out on my
journey from the land of heathenism, superstition, and vice, to a place where the
gospel is preached."

While here he was married to one whose
early experience had been somewhat similar to his own.   His wife, when a little girl,
had been rescued from a slave-ship, and
taken to Sierra Leone, to the same kind
friends who trained him; and they were
brought up together.   When baptized, her
name Asano was changed into Susanna.
In the school at Regent's Town to which
he had been appointed, she was associate
teacher, here and elsewhere filling well
her place in the important and elevated
position to which they had arisen.

Their family of six children, well trained
for usefulness, three of them actively engaged in mission-work, and the others
living godly lives, attest her ability and
faithfulness in the home.

Returning after two years to the Yourah
Bay College, he taught for several years,
doing much good by his influence over the

natives who were being trained there, many of whom were afterward ordained, and appointed to important stations.

In 1841 he made his first trip up the Niger with a party on an exploring expedition planned by the British government in the interest of commerce in native products, which it was hoped would indirectly check the trade in slaves.

Mr. Crowther was sent with this expedition for the purpose of opening the way for the establishing of missions in that region; but on account of a deadly fever which attacked most of the party, they were obliged to return before their mission had been completed. But it was not an entire failure. Friendly relations had been established with the chiefs of various tribes by Mr. Crowther, whose tact and wisdom in dealing with the natives proved that he was the one to push forward the work in the future. During the voyage he prepared a grammar and vocabulary of the Yoruba language, which afterwards was of great value. Upon their return, by request

of the mission at Sierra Leone, he was sent
to London for a year of study, to prepare
him for the ministry; at the close of which
he was ordained, and returned to Africa.
The next year he was sent to his own
country, Yoruba, to establish a mission at
Abbeokuta.   This was a large fortified town
where the Yorubans, after suffering untold
persecutions from the Foulah tribe, had
gathered to the number of a hundred thousand, making a city four miles in diameter.
The people welcomed him with great rejoicing, especially the few Christians among
them who had come hither from Sierra
Leone.   Mr. Crowther had been here about
three weeks when, to his great surprise, he
met his mother and brother, who were
living in a little town near by.   A description of this pathetic scene is given in his
own words, taken from his journal: " We
grasped one another, looking at each other
in great astonishment, big tears rolling
down her emaciated cheeks; she trembled
as she held me by the hand, and called me
by the familiar names with which I well re-

membered I used to be called by my grandmother, who has since died in slavery. We
could not say much, but sat still, and cast
now and then an affectionate look at each
other, — a look which violence and oppression had long checked ; an affection which
had nearly been extinguished by the long
space of twenty-five years. My two sisters
who were captured with us are both with
my mother. Thus unsought for, after all
search for me had failed, God has brought
us together again, and turned our sorrow
into joy."

Two years later she, with three others, became Christians, and were baptized, being
the first fruits of the mission. When baptized, the mother of Samuel took the name
of Hannah. She died in the Christian faith
at the age of ninety-seven. The mission
was blessed with great success, in spite
of terrible persecution by the Juju priests,
and in spite of the continuous wars waged
by the king of Dahomey and his chiefs. Mr.
Crowther wrote at the close of three years :
" What has God wrought during the short

interval of conflict between light and darkness! We have five hundred constant
attendants on the means of grace, about
eighty communicants, and nearly two hundred candidates for baptism; a great number of heathen have ceased worshipping
their country's gods, others have cast theirs
away altogether, and are not far from en-
listing under the banner of Christ."

The missionaries were untiring in their
efforts to help these people, and taught
them to cultivate the soil, and many other
useful employments.

The increased persecutions of the bloodthirsty king of Dahomey made it necessary
for Mr. Crowther again to visit England, in
order to enlist the interest of the English
people in this benighted land, and to ask
their aid in forming an alliance with some
of the surrounding tribes for the suppres-
sion of the slave-trade, and for protection
from these outrages upon the Christians.

While there he completed his dictionary
of the Yoruba language, and his translation
of the Bible into Yoruba. The unusual

ability which he possessed in mastering languages was of the greatest advantage to him in his dealings with the various chiefs.

Having completed his mission in England, he returned to Africa, and continued to extend the work to other localities.

His first mission at Abbeokuta had grown to be a strong centre, with a large and well-built church, in which a congregation of about three hundred natives met for weekly worship. A flourishing school had also been established. Here in conference with the workers from Ibadan and Ijaye, — the outlying stations, — the plans were laid for extending the work in the Yoruba country.

The next three years he spent at Lagos, on the coast, supervising the work there ; and during this time he prepared a primer and vocabulary, and translated several books from the Bible into the Ibo language, thus making preparations for the greater work still before him.

His next expedition up the Niger was planned and sent by the Church Mission-

ary Society. The party consisted of Mr.
Crowther, with two other native ministers,
and two young men who had been living
with one of the missionaries at Sierra
Leone. He had hoped to start six different stations on this trip; but the native
preachers intended to carry on this work
could not be spared on account of the
death of three missionaries on the coast,
so he proceeded with this little band on
the Dayspring; and they had the honor
of planting at Onitsha the first mission on
the great river, which under the care of
the Rev. J. C. Taylor, one of the native
ministers, grew to be a strong centre.

Mr. Crowther now continued his jour-
neyings up and down the river by canoe
or passing boat for five or six years, and
labored with untiring zeal to evangelize
the regions round about. Three other
missions were started as the result of
these labors.

In 1864 he went to England to attend
the annual meeting of the Church Missionary Society, and to report the wonderful

progress already made, and the possibilities for further work, on the Niger. On this visit occurred the most important event in his personal history, when in Canterbury Cathedral, before an immense audience, among whom was the widow of Bishop Weeks, the missionary who had given him his first lessons, he was consecrated first bishop of the Niger.

On his return to Africa his work was resumed with characteristic zeal, his next field being the Delta of the Niger. With his eldest son, archdeacon Dandeson Crowther, as assistant, he established the mission at Bonny, in a region of great degradation, the people being mostly slaves and fetish worshippers, under the power of priests. Many were the victims sacrificed on every possible occasion, and their bones were used to decorate and pave the heathen temples; but under the influence of the gospel, the ghastly temples were deserted, and in the words of the native schoolmaster, wicked Bonny became a bethel. The influence soon spread to Brasse, far-

ther up the river, and another mission was
the result; not, however, without the usual
opposition which always and everywhere
has followed the introduction of Christianity, but which seemed to be unusually
bitter in the Delta regions.

One of the kings who had accepted
Christianity was imprisoned by his chiefs,
and many people were driven to the forests
for safety, who, when they were released,
looked more like skeletons than men ; but
with remarkable fidelity the Christians
adhered to their faith, showing the true
martyr spirit. One, when bribes were offered, said : "As for turning back to heathen worship, that is out of my power; I
have made up my mind to be in chains, if
it so please the Lord, till the judgment
day." Said another, " Jesus has taken
charge of my heart, and padlocked it, and
the key is with him."

Bishop Crowther and his son appealed
to Christians everywhere to pray for them,
so terrible were their sufferings ; and from
all parts of the world letters of sympathy
reached them.

But in spite of persecution, Christianity spread until its influence was felt throughout all the country, and there came in time a complete transformation. Bishop Crowther continued his work on the Niger and throughout the Yoruba country with unabated energy and signal success for more than a quarter of a century, establishing churches and schools, encouraging commerce and agriculture, carrying out most completely the avowed purpose of his youth to spend his life for his people; and in so doing, few have been able to accomplish more than he. Perhaps no part of his work was more important than his many translations of the Bible and other helpful works.

In his several visits to England, he made a multitude of warm friends, who will never forget his kindly, intellectual face, his modest and winning manners. At the World's Missionary Convention held in London in 1888, of the fifteen hundred delegates present from all parts of the world, probably no one received such marked attention as the Black Bishop of the Niger.

On the 31st day of December, 1891, in London, at the age of eighty-two, death removed from earth Bishop Samuel Crowther. His fame, for he was known throughout the world, was not due alone to his singular history, but also to his character and intellectual ability.

Arthur T. Pierson, D.D., in speaking of Bishop Crowther, says : " Wherever he went he brought and left a blessing, and no man perhaps did more than he for the elevation and salvation of his degraded fellow-countrymen. . . . With what joy Mr. Weeks will present to the Lord, Samuel Adjai Crowther, as one of the fruits of his ministry in Africa ! And then for the first time will he realize what ultimate blessing hung on the leading to Christ of an humble slave-boy of Yoruba-land."

X.

JOHN KENNETH MACKENZIE.

Medical Missionary to China.

BORN, AUG. 25, 1850; DIED, APRIL 1, 1888.

X.

JOHN KENNETH MACKENZIE.

AT a recent meeting of the American Board of Commissioners for Foreign Missions, an urgent plea was made by an officer of the association to send more medical missionaries into foreign lands.

The plea was well founded. That a scientific knowledge of medicine may greatly extend the scope of a missionary's work, was clearly shown in the life of John Kenneth Mackenzie.

It is true, medical missions were not new in China when Dr. Mackenzie began his labors in that land; but it is equally true that the attention lately given to Western medicine and surgery by the potentates of the Empire had its origin in the Viceroy's confidence in Dr. Mackenzie's medical skill.

Dr. Mackenzie was born in Yarmouth,

England, Aug. 25, 1850.   His earliest life
was surrounded by the happy influences of
a Christian home.   He was educated for
a time at a private school in Bristol, and
although a quiet, thoughtful boy, had little
real fondness for study, and left school at
the age of fifteen, and became a clerk in a
merchant's office.

While thus employed, young Mackenzie
was a regular attendant at the Young
Men's Christian Association, and in May,
1867, was much impressed by an address
given by Mr. D. L. Moody, then on his
first visit to England.   A year later Mackenzie became a member of the Presbyterian church in Bristol, of which his father
was an elder.

He soon conceived a strong desire to
devote his life to missionary work in China;
and having read " The Double Cure; or,
What is a Medical Mission?" by Mrs. Gordon, believed a medical course would re-en-
force him for labor, and obtained through
the influence of friends his parents' consent to begin the study of medicine with a

view to going to China as a medical missionary. In October, 1870, he entered the Medical School at Bristol, and at the end of four years received his diplomas of M.R.C.S., London, and L.R.C.P., Edinburgh.

He further prepared for his future labor by attendance at the Royal Ophthalmic Hospital in London.

In December, 1874, Dr. Mackenzie wrote to the London Missionary Society, and on the fifteenth of that month received their acceptance of his offers of service for Hankow, and after finishing his studies sailed for that place April 10, 1875, in SS. Glenlyon.

During the voyage Dr. Mackenzie, with the captain's permission, conducted religious services, and entered heartily into whatever made for the benefit and spiritual good of his fellow passengers.

The Glenlyon reached Shanghai June 3, and on the fourth the young doctor embarked upon the Tchang for a trip of six hundred miles up the great Yang-tse-

kiang. The Tchang arrived at Hankow
June 8 ; and Dr. Mackenzie was warmly
welcomed by his future colleagues, Mr.
and Mrs. Griffith John and Mr. Foster.

Hankow, situated at the union of the
Yang-tse and Han rivers, is the great commercial city of Central China ; and the ex-
port tea-trade reaches the figures of three
million pounds sterling a year. Mission
work was established in 1861, when Hankow was opened for foreign trade. In
1866 a hospital and dispensary were added
to the mission ; and later Dr. Reed purchased and gave to the mission a more
healthful site for a new building, which
was erected by native and foreign mer-
chants. This was the field of action to
which Dr. Mackenzie came, and in which
he began his first Sunday by boarding two
of the ten steamers off Hankow, and inviting the sailors to come to the services
on shore. The following Monday found
Dr. Mackenzie at regular attendance at the
hospital in the morning, and hard at the
study of Chinese in the afternoon.

In writing home his impressions of the scenes about him, Dr. Mackenzie said: " It is indeed surprising to see a Chinese city, the streets are so narrow that no such thing as a carriage or cart could possibly get through. In the widest of Hankow streets not more than four or five people could stand abreast. Yet these narrow streets are alive with people all day long; all heavy goods are carried through on wheelbarrows or on coolies' shoulders. The richer people are carried in sedan chairs, and every one has to make way for them. The shops have no windows, but expose their wares directly to the public gaze."

Dr. Mackenzie took a deep interest in the evangelistic work of the Mission, and greatly assisted Mrs. Griffith John in her labor among the sailors. With regard to his special work among the sick, Dr. Mackenzie found much prejudice, and wrote: " The Chinese will only come to us when other help is of no avail." But as days went on the hospital practice greatly increased, and patients at the dispensary multiplied.

In the early fall Dr. Mackenzie, by successful operations, restored vision to two young girls from the interior. The girls were intelligent, and became at once interested in the teachings of Christianity; and through their influence many came to the hospital, not alone that they might be healed of their physical ailments, but that they might learn of the truth. Again, a literary man was healed, and in departing from the hospital took away with him a very complete knowledge of the religion of Christ, and thus gradually the wall of prejudice to foreign innovation, " Christ's greatest stumbling-block," gave way, and Dr. Mackenzie wrote : " For this I am very thankful, for it is my aim to make the hospital a means of proclaiming the gospel and reaching the hearts of the people through kindness and whatever benefit medically one can give them."

Dr. Mackenzie made many journeys with Griffith John into the interior villages, and often met with dangerous persecution from the natives, sometimes being in cities that no Englishman had ever before visited.

As these visits were always fruitful in the healing of physical troubles, as well as in the preaching of God's truth, converts from all parts of the province came to Hankow, and the fame of the skilful Western surgeon spread far and wide. Many diseases hitherto considered incurable were healed, and patients returned home rejoicing. In speaking of medical theories in China, Dr. Mackenzie said : " Chinese doctors profess to be able to diagnose disease by the state of the pulse only. Their knowledge of anatomy and physiology is almost *nil;* yet in place of exact knowledge they substitute the most absurd theories. To a large extent drugs are unknown, and most wonderful healing properties are attributed to such substances as dragon's teeth, fossils, tiger bones, pearls, etc. Moreover, superstitious notions and practices control and pervert medicine. In almost every case of sickness, idols, astrologers, and fortune-tellers are consulted. It is not wonderful, therefore, that medical science being in so unsatisfactory a state in China, the cures wrought by the foreign doctors seem to the people little short of miraculous."

Dr. Mackenzie's practice included all kinds of treatment, from surgery to administration in cases of leprosy. Writing of the opium patients he said : " You will see how the work among opium-smokers has been increased when I give you the following figures. For the first ten months eight persons only agreed to enter the hospital. During the past year, the numbers have increased to two hundred and thirty-five; and during the last month and a half, three hundred and twenty have entered the wards for treatment."

At a later date the doctor wrote that in one year seven hundred persons were treated for opium habits in the Hankow hospital. April 3, 1876, a note in the doctor's diary shows that he then began prayer-meetings for the in-patients. Going to the inland towns whenever he could accompany Mr. John in his evangelistic labors, Dr. Mackenzie learned many Chinese characteristics; and writing of these he said: "The people will tell you, when you ask them what they worship, 'that heaven and earth are greatest and parents the most honorable.' They will not, as a rule, tell you that they worship idols; they have no idea of a Supreme Being. Their contempt for foreigners is very great."

In December, 1876, Dr. Mackenzie went down to Shanghai to meet Miss Travers, the lady to whom he was engaged while in Bristol; and on the ninth they were married in the cathedral by Dean Butcher, and then left at once for their station at Hankow. The young wife entered into the life work of her husband with much enthusiasm, and with him greatly aided in the constant work of Mrs. John among the sailors anchored in Hankow harbor, and with the patients in the hospital.

In August, 1877, Dr. Mackenzie wrote to his mother of a class Mrs. John had

formed to teach a more complete knowledge of the Scriptures to native assistants
and others, and said : " I attended the class
with the object of enlarging my vocabulary;
but I now enjoy the meeting for itself, and
I am as fond of hearing a sermon in Chinese as in English." Oct. 30, 1877, Dr.
and Mrs. Mackenzie rejoiced in the birth
of a daughter. The child was baptized at
the usual Chinese Sunday services by Mr.
John, and named Margaret Ethel.

The winter of 1877–78 was a very severe one in Hankow, and there was much
distress. " One benevolent society alone,"
wrote the doctor, "has given out as many
as one hundred and forty coffins to bury
people found dead in our streets in one
day." Later on the cholera appeared
among the natives; and worn out by incessant labor, Dr. Mackenzie went with his
family to the lakes for a few days rest.

In March, 1879, Dr. Mackenzie was
compelled by family reasons to leave the
Hankow mission and his work, which
had there been physically and spiritually

blessed, and to seek a home farther north. Having asked of, and received from, the London Missionary Society an appointment to Tien-Tsin, Dr. Mackenzie and his family went thither, and were warmly welcomed by Mr. and Mrs. Lees.

Dr. Mackenzie found the mission, from a medical point of view, very far from bright, the institution in charge of a native dispenser, and without funds to buy foreign drugs. Many weary months were passed in earnest prayer to God and man for aid; and at last through the clouds broke a light which will endure for all time, and which afterwards crowned Dr. Mackenzie's labors with success. Royal favor was obtained through the healing of the Viceroy's wife; and His Excellency, convinced of the doctor's skill, set apart an entire quadrangle of one of the finest temples in Tien-Tsin for dispensary work, and contributed £ 200. to purchase drugs for immediate use. Dr. Mackenzie was appointed physician to the royal household, but refused to accept salary for the same, asking rather that the money given might go to the support of the medical work at the temple.

Later, through public subscription, a hospital was erected on vacant space of the London Mission Compound, and the buildings were dedicated by His Excellency Dec. 2, 1880; the occasion was one of special interest, marking an important phase in the history of medical missions in China. Heretofore the work had been carried on by foreign aid, but through the untiring effort of Dr. Mackenzie was now supported from native sources. From the first, Dr. Mackenzie desired to make the hospital free to all who were unable to pay; and from money received for his own personal expenses he immediately started a reserved fund, which, as time went on, was increased by wealthy patients and patrons of the institution; and in December, 1883, Dr. Mackenzie wrote to his brother that he had placed seven thousand taels in trust as a reserve fund, the interest to be used in the work of Christian medical missions.

Ten years before Dr. Mackenzie's work

in Tien-tsin, the Chinese government had sent several lads selected from respectable families to the best schools in America; but in 1881, certain reports having reached the Pekin foreign office that the students were throwing aside the manners and customs of their forefathers, and were in some cases adopting, not only foreign ideas, but foreign religions, a mandate was issued recalling the whole number. Dr. Mackenzie issued a memorial, asking the Viceroy to place eight of these boys under his charge to study medicine, with a view to their becoming medical officers under the government. The proposition was agreed to, and the school inaugurated Dec. 15, 1881.

Feb. 18, 1883, Dr. Mackenzie was obliged to accompany his wife on her second trip to England, as she was now too ill to travel alone. His visit home was passed in awakening interest in the Tien-tsin mission, and in a short visit with his brother to the Continent.

Dr. Mackenzie returned to China Sept. 25, saddened by the separation from his wife, who was not able to accompany him; and the breaking up of his home was a sorrow which shadowed all his after life.

In 1884 the Viceroy sent twelve additional students to the medical school; and under his orders a new hospital was built, and given entirely to the charge of Dr. Mackenzie, who gave great prominence to the evangelistic side of his teaching; thus promoting "The Double Cure," so dear to his heart. In the midst of earnest and successful efforts for all that makes for righteousness, Dr. Mackenzie was stricken with the dread disease, smallpox, and on Easter morning, 1888, rested from his labors.

Dr. Mackenzie sacrificed home, family, life, for his convictions, embodied in the following words: —

"Nothing can save China but Christianity — a heart religion in place of a hollow morality. Once let China awake from her lethargy, moved by the spirit of God, purified and in her right mind, and she will become a mighty power for enduring good."

XI.

JOSEPH HARDY NEESIMA.

Born, Jan. 14, 1843; Died, Jan. 23, 1890.

JOSEPH H. NEESIMA.

XI.

JOSEPH HARDY NEESIMA.

PERHAPS no single private life can better portray genuine Japanese characteristics than that of Joseph Hardy Neesima. In 1843, ten years before Commodore Perry entered the Bay of Yedo, he was born. His father served a prince whose palace was in the city of Yedo.

The feudal system being in existence, boys were preferred to girls in the families of the samurai, as male heirs alone could perpetuate their rank and allowance. Four girls having preceded Neesima, his grandfather hearing of a male born into the family cried "Shimeta!" an exclamation of joy at the realization of some long cherished hope ; and the boy was called Shimeta, the name being written after Neesima, as is usual in Japan.

Neesima's parents were Shintoists, and in his fifth year Neesima was taken to the temple of the god supposed to be his life guardian to offer thanks for his protection. The occasion was a joyous one, and Neesima was as gayly dressed as the heirs of the nobility at an English christening.

Neesima's father was a teacher of penmanship, and many pilgrimages were made to the temple of Japanese hieroglyphics. Several gods were kept in the home, to which the family made offerings. Neesima worshipped these gods until he was fifteen years of age, and then, seeing they did not partake of the food provided for them, refused to do so.

At an early age he developed studious habits, but was very shy, and having some slight impediment in his speech, was sent to a school of etiquette, where he acquired graceful manners and polite conversational style. He was selected by the prince to attend a military school which had been established under the auspices of the Shogun, but later he gave up these exercises and devoted himself to the study of the Chinese classics. Again he was fortunate in being one of three selected to take lessons in Dutch from a native teacher called by the prince to the court to teach his subjects. Afterwards the prince promoted Neesima to the position of assistant teacher in a Chinese school.

Soon after this, Neesima's prince and patron died, and was succeeded by his brother, a man of inferior education. Neesima, now fifteen years of age, was obliged to commence service to the prince, his business being to sit in a little office connected with the front end of the castle and watch the hall, and, with other youths, to bow profoundly as the prince went out or came in, and to pass the rest of the time in gossip and tea-drinking. This life was intolerable to him, and he often planned to escape it by running away from home; but love of family, a strong Japanese characteristic, kept him under his father's roof until he was seventeen years of age, when the war cloud caused by the imperial party rising against the Shogun threw the country into fearful commotion, and Neesima was chosen as a life-guard to his prince. While thus engaged he pursued his studies under great difficulties, but always with untiring persistency; and he was allowed time to go to the Shogun's naval school for lessons in mathematics.   Here one day he caught sight of a Dutch warship lying at anchor in Yedo Bay. "This dignified sea queen," compared with the "clumsy disproportioned Japanese junks," proved an "object lesson" to Neesima; and there was born within him the great desire for the improvement of himself and his country.   The winter of the same year he had an opportunity to go by steamer to Tamashima. This was his first liberation from his prince's "square enclosure," and his first experience with different and individual ideas; his horizon widened, and he was filled with new desires for freedom.

Returning to Yedo, and sympathizing fully with the "imperial party" yet bound by the moral code of Confucius to "the

services of love and reverence to parents,"
Neesima became *distrait* and restless, and
his life might have been entirely perverted
had not destiny intervened. In being asked
of the formative influences of his life,
Neesima, looking back to this time, might
well exclaim with Charles Kingsley, "I
had a friend." This "friend" had a small
library, and among the books proffered for
his use Neesima found a Japanese translation of Robinson Crusoe, and among several
Chinese books an historical geography of
the United States by the Rev. Dr. Bridgman
of the North China Mission, a brief History of the World, written by an English
missionary in China, Dr. Williams's little
magazines, and a few books teaching the
Christian religion, and published at Hong-
Kong or Shanghai. Speaking of these
books, Mr. Neesima in later life said, "I
read them with close attention. I was partly
a sceptic, and partly struck with reverential
awe. I became acquainted with the name
of the Creator through those Dutch books
I had studied before; but it never came

home so dear to my heart as when I read the simple story of God's creation of the universe on those pages of a brief Chinese Bible History.   I found out that the world we live upon was created by his unseen hand, and not by mere chance.   I discovered in the same history that his other name was the 'Heavenly Father,' which created in me more reverence towards him, because I thought he was more to me than a mere Creator of the world.   All these books helped me to behold a Being, somewhat dimly yet, in my mental eye, who was so blindly concealed from me during the first two decades of my life."

At this time no missionaries were allowed in Japan.   So Neesima, recognizing God as the only father to whom he owed life fealty, determined to break the environments of his youth, and to leave temporarily his home and country.   With some difficulty he obtained first his prince's, then his parents', sanction to leave Yedo, ostensibly to go to Hakodate, and in the spring of 1864 went thither.   Neesima, always thinking of his country and its conditions, watched closely the people of Hakodate, and, painfully cognizant of their corrupt existence, determined that Japan needed moral reformation more than mere material progress. His desire to visit a foreign land he confided to a Japanese clerk employed by an English merchant. This friend at midnight and with great difficulty conveyed Neesima in a row-boat alongside an American vessel, whose kind-hearted captain had consented to take the Japanese boy as far as China. At Shanghai, Neesima was transferred to the American ship Wild Rover, whose captain employed Neesima to wait upon the table; and not liking "Shimeta," called "his boy" Joe, and was uniformly kind to him. After a four months' voyage the ship reached Boston Harbor, and through the kind interest of Captain Taylor, Neesima was introduced to the owner of the Wild Rover, Mr. Alpheus Hardy, one of Boston's noblest philanthropists.

He became at once interested in the

boy, and, with Mrs. Hardy, assumed the responsibility of his education. In September, 1865, he entered the English department of Phillips Academy, Andover. Here he remained until 1867, when his benefactors sent him to Amherst. His letters during his student life tell of frequent illnesses, which at times interfered with his work, of his tramps through different States during vacation, of letters from his Japanese parents, of his anxiety about his home affairs during the rise of the princes against the shogun in 1868–1869, of his growing spirituality, and of his heartfelt gratitude to Mr. and Mrs. Hardy.

In a letter dated March 21, 1871, Neesima writes that he met in Boston, Mori, the Japanese minister sent to Washington by the mikado. Mr. Mori offered to reimburse Mr. Hardy for Neesima's educational expenses, and thereby make Neesima subject to Japanese government. Mr. Hardy at once declined the proposition. On Sept. 17, 1871, Neesima wrote to Mrs. Hardy that he had received a passport from the

Japanese government, and that from the same source his father had received a paper saying: "It is permitted by the government to Neesima Shimeta to remain and study in the United States of America." In 1872 an embassy representing the imperial government of the mikado visited America and Europe on visits of inquiry into Western civilization; and Minister Mori summoned Mr. Neesima to Washington to meet the embassy, and to assist Mr. Tanaka, the commissioner of education. In this way Mr. Neesima became acquainted with the most progressive men of new Japan, whose friendship in later years was of great value to him. Fearing, however, that his plan to return to Japan as a free advocate of Christianity might be endangered, he carefully stipulated that Mr. Mori should state to the embassy that any service desired of him would be undertaken only under a contract that freed him from all obligation to the Japanese government.

Under these circumstances he was engaged, and soon proved so valuable an assistant, that Mr. Tanaka insisted upon his accompanying the embassy to Europe. There he gave all his time to the study of the best methods of learning in schools and institutions of all grades; and on the basis of his reports was built to-day's educational system in Japan, From this European trip with the embassy Mr. Neesima returned to Andover in September, 1873.

In March, 1874, Mr. Neesima formally offered himself to the American Board, and July 2 was appointed corresponding member to the Japanese mission. He was graduated as a special student from Andover Theological Seminary, and ordained in Boston, September 24.

The Board held its sixty-fifth annual meeting at Rutland, Vt., that autumn, and Mr. Neesima spoke on the establishment of a Christian college in Japan. By his soul-felt enthusiasm the young Japanese carried his audience with him; $5,000 was at once subscribed, and Neesima's dream became a reality.

In October, after an absence of ten years, Neesima left New York for his native land. The changes that had taken place there seemed to him almost incredible. He found a national line of steamers, lighthouses at all important coast points, a general telegraphic system, a postal service, an organized navy, and a railway between Yokohama and the capital. In the treaty ports small Protestant churches had been established; but in visiting his parents at Annoka, directly after his arrival in Japan, Neesima was the first to carry the gospel to the interior, and here he founded one of the most genuinely Christian communities in Japan.

Neesima arrived at Osaka, the home of the American Board Mission, Jan. 22, and here he planned to establish a Christian school with a broad collegiate course; but meeting with opposition, he gave up the project, and turned his steps towards Kyoto. Here he met with many and varied difficulties, but by persistent effort opened, Nov. 25, 1875, the Doshisha, with eight pupils. The winter of 1875 was one of hardship and discouragement; but assisted by the Rev. J. D. Davis, D.D., he maintained the school, which constantly increased in numbers.

On Jan. 2, 1876, Neesima was married to the sister of the counsellor to the Kyoto Fu. She had been a teacher in the government school for girls, but her engagement to a Christian caused her discharge.

After her marriage she entered fully into her husband's life-work; and in their house, provided by Mr. J. M. Sears of Boston, services were constantly held, and Christian teaching promulgated.

From 1876 to 1884 Mr. Neesima's life was filled with trials, and obstacles of every kind threatened the very existence of the Doshisha. The fact that the school, while nominally a Japanese company, was in reality supported from foreign means, caused an attack which compelled Mr. Neesima to write to the Prudential Committee for a permanent endowment; and in November, 1879, he received the joyful tidings that the year's appropriation of eight thousand dollars would soon be placed under his direction for the educational work in Kyoto.

The keynote of true teaching was struck by Mr. Neesima's effort to disseminate Christianity through an educated ministry. In 1880 he writes: " Try to send out choice men, — Christians must not be charged with being ignoramuses, — or we shall be ridiculed for our lack of learning as well as for our faith. We need the broadest culture and Christian spirit to counteract the downward tendency of our educated youth."

Through all his work Mr. Neesima entertained the hope born at Andover of a Christian university at Japan, and determined to raise endowments for history, philosophy, political economy, law, and medicine. His personal activity in this direction was incessant ; but, his health failing, he accepted in 1884 an invitation for rest and change from the Board, and visited Europe and America. During this trip he everywhere inspected schools and colleges, and noted in detail methods and results, and made plans of buildings and apparatus.

He arrived in Boston, Sept. 27, 1884; but even there he was not freed from care and responsibilities. The outlook in Japan was broadening, and the demand great to place the Doshisha upon a university basis; and he was looked upon as the medium between Japan and the source of its supply. In December it became necessary for him to go to Clifton Springs, N.Y., for rest at the Sanitarium. He left there in March, 1885, somewhat better in health, and cheered by the news that fifty thousand dollars had been appropriated for the Japan mission. He arrived at Yokohama Dec. 12, 1885, "and found five hundred friends, students, teachers, relatives, and prominent citizens," assembled there to meet him. The day after this the tenth anniversary of the Doshisha was celebrated, and the corner-stone of two new buildings laid. The school was in a flourishing condition; and the Japanese boy of long ago was now, by acclamation of its faculty, president of the college.

Two years later Amherst College conferred upon Neesima the degree of doctor of laws. May 17, 1887, an income of not less than twenty-five hundred dollars per annum was assured to the Doshisha by the American Board. In April, 1888, a meeting was held in the great Buddhist temple of Chionin in Kyoto, to consider the question of a university endowment. In July a dinner was given to Mr. Neesima by the late minister of foreign affairs, that he might present this question to distinguished Japanese guests. At this dinner Mr. Neesima fainted, worn out by his efforts. The result of the meeting was a pledge of thirty thousand dollars to the university. In the summer of 1888 he was told by his physicians that he had not long to live, and by their advice was taken to a mountain resort (Ikao) ; here he was cheered by the gift to the Doshisha of a hundred thousand dollars from Mr. J. N. Harris of New London, Conn. Writing to

Mr. Harris, Mr. Neesima says, "A dona-
tion like this is unknown and unprece-
dented in our country."

During the summer months of 1889
Neesima's health seemed to improve; and
after seeing the foundation for the new
science building laid, he went to Tokyo to
work for the endowment fund; but rest
was again advised by his physicians, and
he went to Oiso; and here, Jan. 23, 1890,
he died.

On the news of Mr. Neesima's dangerous illness, the students of Doshisha were
with difficulty restrained from proceeding
in a body to his bedside. On Jan. 24
the body was taken to Kyoto, where the
funeral services took place, Jan. 27, in
presence of the school, graduates from all
parts of the empire, city authorities, and
representatives of foreign missions. In the
procession (a mile and a half in length)
was seen a delegation of priests bearing
the inscription, "From the Buddhists of
Osaka." Truly no private citizen ever
died in Japan whose loss was so widely

and so deeply felt as that of Mr. Neesima. On the plain below Kyoto stands his outward monument, the Doshisha, from whose walls have come the most powerful factors in the civilization of new Japan; but in the lives of the men about him is written the endurance of his influence, the divinity of his soul.

XII.

JOHN WILLIAMS.

The martyr missionary of Polynesia.

Born June 27, 1796.   Died Nov. 20, 1839.

XII.

JOHN WILLIAMS.

THE story of the life and ministry of John Williams will ever occupy a prominent place in the history of missions ; for to the intense devotion and zeal which he brought to his work was added an originality of method which has benefited all who came after him.

In early life there were no marked indications of the part he was to take in the great work of the world's evangelization.

He was suddenly brought to a decision, and his life instantly changed from one of aimless indifference to that of enthusiastic activity, with a distinct and determined purpose in view, to the accomplishment of which he brought to bear all of his genius and attractive personality.

He was born June 27, 1796, in the same

year, and within a few weeks of the time,
that the London Missionary Society sent
out the first missionary to the South Sea
Islands.   This band of thirty missionaries
sailed in the Duff, Aug. 10, 1796.

In the little village of Tottenham, England, six miles north of London, he was
born, and lived until fourteen years of age,
when it was thought by his parents time
for him to begin his business training ; and
he was apprenticed to an ironmonger in
London for seven years.   From this contract he was released at the end of six
years to take up his great work in the
South Seas.

Life in a great city then, as now, was
a severe test of the Christian character
of a young lad ; and after four years of
its diversions and temptations, we find him
at eighteen drifting with the multitude.

He was standing one Sunday evening
on a street corner, waiting for some companions who were to meet him there, and
go with him to the Highbury Tea-Gardens, when a lady, the wife of his em-

ployer, on her way to church, passed ;
recognizing him, she turned back and asked
him to go to church. He refused, but she
felt constrained to urge ; her persistence,
and the failure of his chums to appear,
decided him, and with reluctance he accompanied her to the old Whitefield Tabernacle. The sermon from the text, " What
shall it profit a man if he gain the whole
world and lose his own soul ?" proved to
be the word in season ; for he went out
from the house a new creature, immediately forsaking his worldly companions
and sinful ways.

He became a teacher in the Sunday-
school, and at once entered upon a new
and higher life, availing himself of every
means for self-improvement which would
better fit him for usefulness in his Christian life.

To his success in this direction very
much credit is due the Rev. Matthew Wilks,
then pastor of the Tabernacle. Mr. Wilks
was an eloquent preacher, full of missionary zeal, a faithful pastor, with a keen

discernment of character, which led him to see in John Williams capabilities for great usefulness, and to invite him to join a class of young men whom he then had under instruction for the ministry. These studies were continued for two years, until his appointment by the London Missionary Society.

It was customary in this church, which stood foremost in missionary enthusiasm of any in London, to have quarterly missionary meetings; and it was at one of these meetings that John Williams felt his first call to the work. Soon after he sent his application, with these words: " If this, and the account which the Rev. Matthew Wilks can give of me, should not meet with your approval, I hope and pray that you will on no account for the sake of my soul offer me the least encouragement."

He, with eight others, one of whom was the noted Robert Moffat, were ordained and set apart to the missionary ministry, in Surrey Chapel, London, on the 30th of September, 1816.

It was at first intended that John Williams and Robert Moffat should go out together, but objection was made on account of the extreme youthfulness of both. In the words of the Rev. Dr. Waugh: " Tha twa callants were ower young ta gang t'gether." But Mr. Williams found a companion before going. He was married to Miss Mary Chauner, a young lady in the same church, of devoted Christian character, who had long cherished the desire to be a missionary; and she was to him, through all of his varied and hazardous experiences, a strong support.

The young husband, with his pretty, girlish-looking bride, sailed with other missionaries for the South Seas on the 17th of November, 1816; and exactly twelve months from that date landed at Eimeo, one of the Society group.

His active mind and ready hands were never at a loss for something to do; and he proceeded to build a boat, which he saw was greatly needed by both missionaries and natives. This was the first of five boats built by him during his nineteen years of ministry on these islands. In ten months he had, by a method of his own, mastered the difficult language, which usually took three years, and was ready to preach to the natives.

At this time there came to the mission a call from the neighboring island of Huahine for teachers; and Mr. Williams, with two other missionaries and their wives, responded to the call, and started a new mission there.

It was not long, however, before a call came to this mission from the island of Raiatea. Tamatao, the king, who came with the message, had been converted to Christianity while on a visit to Tahiti, and on returning had induced some of his subjects to join him; but they had been sorely persecuted on account of their faith, and when they came to the missionaries for help, it was decided that Mr. Williams should go with King Tamatao to his beautiful island. Here dates the beginning of his remarkably successful career of misƒionary labors, extending to so large a number of those benighted peoples. With Raiatea of the Society group as his first centre or base of operations, Raratonga of the Hervey group as his second, and Upolu of the Samoan group as his third, he was able to spread the gospel to most of the islands in each of these groups.

He was planning a similar work among the New Hebrides, and had gone there intending to start a fourth mission centre on the island of Erromango at the time of his sudden and tragic death.

It is said that after eighteen years the gospel had through his instrumentality been given to a population of about three hundred thousand, while many more had felt the uplifting benefits of civilization which he had so skilfully introduced among them.

Raiatea was considered a very important point, being both a religious and political centre. The work here was, as at other points, wonderfully successful, by reason of his personal power in drawing the natives to himself, and his wisdom and tactful management of them.

His teaching was comprehensive; and they were not only instructed in spiritual things, but to an unusual extent were trained in the arts of civilization. Captains of ships visiting the islands were unanimous in their praise of the character of his work.

His first step here was to draw the natives together from their isolated homes, where they were living in hostility, into a settlement, giving then an object-lesson in the building of his own house. The plastered walls, decorated with coloring obtained from the coral, and the sofas, chairs, and tables of his own manufacture, all greatly interested them. The king and others were induced to follow his example, until very soon there was a little town of one thousand, extending two miles along the coast.

Aiming always to keep them busy, he stimulated them to activity by various means. He built another boat, ingeniously tying the planks together with native cord, then offering fifty nails to the one who would make one like it.

He also erected a sugar-mill for the use of the natives, and encouraged the culture of the native cane. They soon had many plantations under cultivation, and various products for transportation.

When the increasing number of Christians made it necessary to build a new chapel, they were also prepared to take another step in civilization.

This new church building was a unique structure, in that it had an apartment for a court-room, in which, the day after the dedication, when twenty-four hundred persons were present, the people again convened and adopted a code of laws which he had prepared for them. The vote for adoption was unanimous, and the brother of Tamatao was appointed chief justice.

Their language was reduced to writing, and schools established, into which were gathered hundreds of children.

Mr. Williams gave special attention to

the training of natives as teachers and leaders, sending them out to do pioneer work on other islands, under his direction. Mr. Williams had rare qualities for this supervisory work, and also the ability to select those who were capable of doing the work.

His son calls attention to the fact that "he was the first of our modern missionaries so to use native agents." This method has been extensively adopted by the missionaries who followed him, and their success proves the wisdom of it.

His heart was continually going out to those beyond him. He could not content himself within the narrow limits of one little reef, and he made frequent visits to neighboring islands.

He said, "Had I a ship at my command, not an island in the Pacific but should, God permitting, be visited, and teachers sent to direct the wandering feet of the heathen to happiness and to heaven."

At one time, being obliged to go to

Sydney for medical treatment, he, with permission of the Missionary Societies' agent,
bought a ship, which he loaded with food,
clothing, and useful articles for the islanders, also some sheep, cows, and a present
from the governor to the island chiefs.
He also engaged a man to go with him
to teach the natives agriculture. In this
vessel, which he named the Endeavor, he
returned to Raiatea with great joy. By
using it as a trading-vessel, he would
be able to keep away other ships which
brought nothing but evil. He called them
" the very arks of Satan," and considered
the Endeavor a profitable investment, if
only to keep these away. By it also he
would get beyond his one little reef, and
begin on his cherished project of planting
a mission on every island of the Pacific.

He made one tour on the Endeavor,
taking six native teachers, who were left
on different islands, and discovered Raratonga, which later became his home for
a time. In his journal at this time we
read : " I hope for great things, pray for

great things, and confidently expect great things."

But much to his disappointment and sorrow, and contrary to his judgment, the directors of the London Missionary Society decided that a ship was not a necessary part of a missionary's outfit, and the Endeavor was sold.

They did not understand then as they did later the breadth and scope of the work he had in mind.

When the mission at Raiatea was well established, he transferred his home and labors to Raratonga, of the Hervey group.

Here, as elsewhere, he won all hearts by his strong personality, and by the stimulating example of his ceaseless activity was able to do for them all that had been accomplished at Raiatea ; so that the mission at Raratonga became a stronghold, sending out its trained workers to all of the adjacent islands.

The natives of the Samoan Islands had long been considered the most savage of any in the South Seas ; and John Williams, for this reason, no doubt, had had for several years a great desire to carry the gospel to them. When, therefore, the enterprise at Raratonga was in turn sufficiently established, he felt the renewed call to go to Samoa so strongly that he could no longer resist; and with what seems to us an inspiration from above, he went to work to build a ship large enough to carry him on this long journey of two thousand miles. This feat has been looked upon as bordering on the miraculous, from the fact that he had neither machinery nor materials to work with.

He named this vessel the Messenger of Peace; and in it, after visiting all the islands where he had succeeded in starting the work, he proceeded on his way to Samoa.

We cannot in this condensed sketch go into the details of this interesting voyage. Suffice it to say, that the same methods were followed that had been employed on previous smaller tours; viz., teachers were left wherever it was thought to be safe; and where the savage condition of the natives rendered this impossible, efforts were made to induce a few of them to come on board the ship, to go to some neighboring island, where every means would be used to instruct them in the truth, so that when he returned to his home again, a little seed might be sown, and later it might be possible to place a teacher with them.

The way seemed to open before him; and in less than two years from this first visit to Samoa, a complete change had taken place in the savage Samoans, — chapels were built, and schools were established everywhere.

Having now spent seventeen years in this arduous work, and feeling the need of change, he, with his family, consisting of his wife and two sons, returned to England, where he spent four years, which were considered by many quite as fruitful of good as any spent in the South Sea. During this time he wrote two books, had the Raratongan New Testament printed, spoke to many large audiences, and raised

£4,000 for the purchase of a missionary ship, and for the establishment of a college at Tahiti for the education of native teachers.

In 1838 he and his wife again embarked for the South Seas, taking ten other missionaries in the Camden (the ship which had been purchased for him in London), landing at Upolu, which place he then considered his home. He spent a few months here, and then made a tour of all the stations where he had established missions on the Society and Hervey Islands, being gone over four months. After a few months of rest and preparation at Upolu, he started on what he called his "great voyage" to the New Hebrides. For some reason he seemed to be unusually impressed in the anticipations of this undertaking, and looked upon it as more important than anything he had yet accomplished. At his farewell sermon the day before starting, Nov. 3, 1839, all were deeply affected. On the sixteenth, when within sixty miles of the New Hebrides, he wrote in a letter to a friend, " We shall be there early to-morrow morning. This evening we are to have a special prayer-meeting. Oh, how much depends upon the efforts of to-morrow! *Will the savages receive us or not?* Perhaps at this moment you or some other kind friend may be wrestling with God for us. I am all anxiety. . . . I brought twelve missionaries with me; two have settled at a beautiful island of Rotuma; the ten are for the New Hebrides and New Caledonia. The approaching week is to me the most important of my life."

They stopped at two islands, but did not land, and endeavored to create such friendly feeling that in the near future they might be able to land and leave teachers. Landing at Port Resolution, they had, in Mr. Williams's words, " one of the most interesting visits we have yet been privileged to have with the heathen in their barbarous and savage state." Thence on to fatal Erromanga, dark Erromanga. So intense was his anxiety in regard to future developments, that he slept very little the night previous, and on this night made the last entry in his diary as follows : —

MONDAY, A. M., 18TH. — This is a memorable day . . . and the records of the events will exist after those who have taken an active part in them have retired into the shades of oblivion; and *the results of this day will be*"— These were the last words he ever wrote.

Landing at Dillon's Bay, Captain Morgan thus described the island : " The shore looked most inviting, placid stillness swept along the romantic rocks, and the mountains in the distance presented a most enchanting scene."

Encouraged by their previous friendly reception, they ventured to go out among the natives who were gathering in groups on the shore, Mr. Williams and Mr. Harris going some distance, carrying presents and making friendly advances. Suddenly there was a terrible yell, and Mr. Harris was seen running, the savages after him. Captain Morgan and Mr. Cunningham, who were near the boat, barely escaped, but the others were stricken down.

Mr. Williams succeeded in reaching the beach, and the waters of the bay were colored with the blood from his wounds; and here would that we could say that the bereaved ones on the ship had the Christian privilege of tenderly caring for the bodies of their dead comrades, giving that little comfort to the breaking heart of her who now all unconscious of the terrible fate was patiently awaiting the coming of her loved one; but this dark picture has no such relief, for the Erromangas were cannibals.

On a tablet in Apia in Samoa is this inscription: " Sacred to the memory of the Rev. John Williams, Father of the Samoan and other missions, aged 43 years and 5 months, who was killed by the cruel natives of Erromanga, on November 20, 1839, while endeavoring to plant the Gospel of Peace on their shores."

XIII.

ROBERT W. LOGAN.

Missionary to Micronesia.

Born May 4, 1843; Died Dec. 27, 1887.

XIII.

ROBERT W. LOGAN.

ROBERT WILLIAM LOGAN was born in York, Medina County, Ohio, May 4, 1843. His parents were from Scotland, and settled upon a new farm on this portion of the Western Reserve. Here they spent their strength and lives in the toil incident to making a home in the comparative wilderness of this new country. Both parents died when Robert was quite young, and he grew up under the care of elder brothers and a sister.

He was gentle, sunny-tempered, and obliging, which led him to be a favorite among his school-fellows, while his natural ability as a scholar made him equally a favorite with his teachers. From a child, something beyond the ordinary seems to have been expected of him, both intellec-

tually and morally.   He was wont to
say sometimes in the later years of his life,
that had there been some wise friend to
direct his reading and study in those
earlier years, he might perhaps have made
his mark as a scholar; but as he grew to
manhood one thing and another occurred
to prevent his giving his time to study.
He went to Wisconsin, where some of the
older members of the family had settled,
and where for a time he assisted his
brother in farmwork during the summer,
and taught school in winter.

While there the War of the Rebellion
broke out, and he, with an older brother, en-
listed.   He was young, and his family and
friends felt quite unwilling to have him go;
but he felt that his country needed and
called him, and the call could not be put
aside.   His brother said of him at this
time, " Robert always does things from a
sense of duty, and it is of no use to try to
turn him aside if he feels that he ought
to go."   His service as a soldier was not a
long one, but it came near costing him his

life. It did, indeed, cost him the vigor of all the more mature years of his manhood; for he was never strong or robust after his army experience, and it would seem that without doubt his life was shortened by it.

After partially regaining his health, he sought to go on with his studies, but was again prevented, this time by the long and painful illness of a maternal uncle, who called him to his bedside, where he remained caring for him and his interests during a period of about three years.

It was during the third year of his life with his uncle that he was led to take a decided stand for Christ, and to identify himself with God's people. I do not think this new step made any great change in his outward life. He had always been faithful and conscientious towards all the claims which he had recognized; it needed but a few words from one or two faithful friends to show him God's claim upon him and his life, and he at once recognized that claim, and yielded to it in a new and glad surrender.

With this new motive in his life, there came new thoughts and plans. God had a work for him to do, and he had to prepare for it. He was now twenty-three years old. He regretted that he had not heard the call sooner, and begun his work of preparation earlier, that it might have been more thorough ; but he wasted no time in vain regrets. He went at once to Oberlin, and began his work as a student. His life in Oberlin brought him in contact with those who realized to him his ideals of noble Christian manhood, and stimulated in him his purpose of giving his life for the good of others.

The question of foreign missionary service was not brought decidedly before him until the early part of his last year in the seminary. It was fully decided at that time ; but at the time of his graduation his health seemed so broken that it was not thought advisable for him to go abroad. A year later he saw in the *Missionary Herald* an urgent plea for helpers from the veteran missionary Sturges at Ponape,

Micronesia. He was much improved in health, and at once wrote to Secretary Clark at Boston, saying, "Here am I; send me."

The intervening winter was a busy one. There was no medical missionary in the Micronesian field then, and it was thought advisable that Mr. Logan should obtain some practical knowledge of medicine; so the time during the week was spent in one of the medical schools in Cleveland, Ohio, and he preached on Sundays. The practical knowledge of medicine which he obtained that winter was of immense value for his own family and the families of his associates as well as for what he was able to do for the natives.

He was united in marriage to Miss Mary E. Fenn, also of York, Ohio, May 4, 1870. Mrs. Logan was well trained for the work, and was very helpful in every branch of the missionary service, especially in teaching and translating. She shared the hardships and perils of her husband like a true heroine, and continued in that difficult and isolated field several years after Mr. Logan's death.

Mr. and Mrs. Logan landed on the island of Ponape in September, 1874, after a voyage of some ten weeks from Honolulu; a voyage which was something of preparation for those which came later, full of stern realities, of seasickness, of visions of naked savages, and of a home among them at its close.

The work on Ponape at that time was in a transition period. It had been the popular thing, both among chiefs and people, to leave the old form of religion, and to put one's self on a footing with the new. Thus many had come into the church who understood little of the spiritual meaning of the new life. During the years which followed, there was the painful and laborious sifting process, the falling away of those whose hearts had not been really touched; and also the brighter and more joyous, if not less laborious, work of aiding to build up in character and spiritual strength those who were really of the kingdom.

The foreign missionary work from the island of Ponape had been begun by Mr. Sturges and Mr. Doane in 1874, by taking to the Mortlock Islands, three hundred miles west of Ponape, three men and their wives, who had received some training, to commence a work among a people speaking a different dialect, who had never yet heard the gospel of Christ. The story of the devotion and faith and skill of these men and women, who were but just out of heathenism themselves, and the wonderful way in which God used them to make known his name and power, is no new story to-day to those who have watched the work in Micronesia.

Mr. Logan's connection with this work began in 1878, when he made his first visit to that interesting field with Mr. Sturges. The original three Ponape families had been re-enforced by others, and the work had spread to other islets and lagoons. Churches had been built, schools were in progress, almost the entire population of something more than five thousand had largely put away their heathen customs, and were sitting at the feet of their teachers.

These teachers had reduced the language to writing. They had translated some Christian hymns from their own Ponape dialect into this new one, and also a small reading-book. This was literally all they had with which to feed the multitude.

There was a mighty work to be done, and it had to be done quickly. The King's business requires haste. These famishing, hungry ones must not be left a day nor an hour longer than necessity required, lest they turn again to the beggarly elements of heathenism to satisfy their soul-hunger; and these men and women who were showing themselves worthy to be used of God must have tools with which to work.

These were something of the thoughts and motives which moved Mr. Logan to ask at once of the mission at Ponape that he be designated to learn the Mortlock language in connection with his regular station work. His study of the language the first year was with Mortlock people who had come to Ponape to attend school; but the following year Mr. and Mrs. Logan took up their residence temporarily on one of the Mortlock Islands, where Mr. Logan carried on his work of translating and bookmaking.

He always worked easily and rapidly; his mind was quick and alert, speedily arriving at conclusions which others reached only after a much longer and more laborious process. He was wont to say of his translation of the New Testament, " There are mistakes ; he who comes after me will find them, I know. It could not be otherwise in doing my work so entirely without advice and counsel; but, on the other hand, it is from the original, and I am sure it is reasonably correct."

Nor was the translating his only work during their stay at the Mortlock Islands. The touring and general supervision were important and helpful factors in a work which had received so little direct supervision as had this; and it would be diffi-

cult to express in a few words what he was
to those native teachers. Quick to grasp
the situation and to read native character,
with a large, loving, and sympathetic heart,
he was at once to them elder brother, ad-
viser, faithful friend, and physician. He
wrought with them, and ever stimulated
them to do their best work for the Master.

Perhaps no greater test of their faith
and Christian fortitude ever came to these
missionaries than while on this desolate
coral island at this period they awaited the
coming of the Morning Star which had
been long delayed. Mr. Logan had had
a sudden and severe attack of hemor-
rhage of the lungs, and seemed to be rapidly sinking. Their supply of food was
almost exhausted ; and Mrs. Logan, unable to get for him the nourishment he
needed, had to endure that most painful or-
deal of waiting and watching in utter help-
lessness. As the long, hot days brought
no relief, and still no signs of the Morning
Star appeared, they were finally obliged to
accept the kindly offer of passage on a little

trading-vessel that touched at the island, and conveyed them to New Zealand. The kind-hearted sailors put up a temporary awning on the little deck, to give the suffering missionary some protection from the tropical sun, and shared with the stricken family their coarse fare. But through all these sufferings and privations there were no murmurings or expressions of bitterness from this noble man, whose spirit reminds those who knew him well of John the beloved disciple.

Returning ·to America, his stay of two years was marked by two important events, — the printing of two books in the Mortlock language, the New Testament and a book of Bible history ; and a gradual return to a measure of health and vigor, so that it was deemed expedient for him to venture upon a return to the loved work in Micronesia.

Mr. and Mrs. Logan reached the Ruk lagoon in October, 1884, after a weary voyage of ten weeks. This great lagoon lies four hundred miles west of Ponape, and its fifteen thousand people speak the same language as the Mortlock people. The work previously commenced in the Mortlock Islands had spread on to the westward, until it had reached Ruk in 1880, since which time an intelligent and faithful native missionary from Ponape, named Moses, had, with several associate workers, been striving to bring some rays of light into the appalling darkness of heathenism which reigned there.

The Ruk people, though speaking essentially the same language as the Mortlock people, and evidently of the same family, were far more fierce and bloodthirsty. They had had little intercourse with the outside world, for navigators and traders were afraid of them. They had little regard for human life, none for the property of others, and lived in a constant state of fear and warfare.

Mr. Logan found here the beginnings of a real work. The life and teachings of Moses and his associates had been such as to make a very favorable impression upon the people; and there was on several islands of the lagoon an earnest desire for the coming of more missionaries and for the spread of their teachings. Mr. and Mrs. Logan began their life and work among them under comparatively favorable circumstances and with high hopes.

Those who have had no experience in such a life can form little idea of its surroundings or its isolation. Shut off from the outside world, and hearing from it very infrequently, surrounded by these degraded, superstitious, naked people, realizing again and again how entirely the lives of missionaries were in their hands, yet feeling that they were indeed brothers and sisters for whom Christ died, they felt that they had a great responsibility as well as a great privilege.

Mr. Logan realized this responsibility and privilege most keenly, and these three last years of his life were given up to the work with an utter abandonment of self which would have been impossible in a less intense nature than his. Morning and evening meetings, school and church work,

going about by boat or canoe to the different islands in the lagoon, settling quarrels,
medical work, making school-books, were
some of the many demands upon his time
and strength; and added to all, the going
out of the heart in intense sympathy and
love to these who were in so great darkness, and the ever-increasing burden of the
things which must be done in laying foundations for the fair and wondrous structure
of Christianity. During those three short
years he came to wield a mighty influence
over them because they loved him, knowing that he loved them.

Wise economy, indeed, would it have
been for the churches at home to supple-
ment the years and the strength of this
wise and loving worker with faithful, energetic, and efficient helpers; not suffering
him to be crushed beneath the heavy load
of toil and care. Well had it been for the
work could he have realized that his frail,
suffering body was no match for his daunt-
less spirit.

He entered into the rest of God's people Dec. 27, 1887. As he lay on his dying bed, he said to Mrs. Logan, "You must go home to America, and tell some of the young and earnest workers to come and take up this work." In her loneliness, grief, and agony she replied, "How can I ask others to come and suffer as we are suffering now?" With the light of heaven in his face he answered, "It is God's work, and it is worth all it costs." O Man of Sorrows! his Master and Saviour and ours, surely this was the thought of thy heart when thou didst hang upon the Cross, "It is my Father's work, and it is worth all it costs."

The Rev. Frank S. Fitch, D.D., of Buffalo, N.Y., a classmate in Oberlin College, gave the following beautiful tribute to the memory of the Rev. Robert W. Logan, at the meeting of the American Board in Cleveland, 1888 : —

"I only bring a sprig of laurel to drop on the scarcely closed grave of one who was not only my friend, but the friend of many in Ohio; and I am sure that it is meet that we should pause for a moment in the midst of the pressing affairs of the present, and the great outreach for the future, to pay this tribute of respect to one of the most honored and most successful of our modern mis-sionaries.

" When he offered himself for service to the Board, the only suggestion he made as regards his place, was that he might be sent to that place for which it was most difficult to find any one. He had, as his instructors have told me, given evidence of far more than the average degree of intellectual ability, and might have filled important positions at home. But there was in him, in the midst of a very quiet and unassuming manner, a quality of heroism which I myself have not seen equalled. The eight thou-sand miles of distance, the isolation of those islands, where a mail is received but once in six months, the most utter absence of such food as that to which we are accustomed, and the lack of all stimulus from neighboring surroundings, made this field difficult enough, certainly, even for his chival-ric spirit. And yet he persisted for years in this work, and came home some six years ago so en-tirely disabled that it seemed to all his friends that it was cruelty to allow him to return. And yet he felt called upon to return, and his remaining years were years full of remarkable fruitage.

He was a very gifted missionary in the direct work of the missionary, and he also did great work as a translator. Perhaps his greatest power, if we

judge him by his intellectual gifts, was the gift
which he exercised in the control of those who were
subordinate to him, — the native helpers and the
native chiefs. He was able to quell insurrection,
and bring haughty chiefs to obedience ; and he has
therein accomplished a work which we shall long
remember. All who have had relations to him will
be made the richer for all time and for all eternity
by the influence that has come from his heroism,
his patience, his unfaltering faith."

XIV.

WILLIAM BUTLER.

Missionary to India and Mexico.

BORN, 1818.

WILLIAM BUTLER.

XIV.

WILLIAM BUTLER.

IT was the happy Christian experience of an old blind harper that forged the first visible link in the chain of providences which brought William Butler from a life of careless ease to the work of preaching the gospel. The poor sightless musician doubtless felt that he could do very little for the Master he loved, — naught save to testify of his goodness; yet God honored his quiet, consistent life by giving him thus a share in the work of bringing the world to the feet of Christ.

William Butler was born in Ireland in 1818. Early left an orphan, he was for some years in the care of a godly great-grandmother, who used to induce the little lad to mount a chair for a pulpit, and, clad in an improvised surplice, to read

the lessons for the day from the Church of
England Prayer-book.   This little service
was a great comfort to the venerable old
lady, who was unable longer to attend
church.   In his early manhood, however,
he lived without any serious aim in life,
until the question, " Do you pray ? " was
put to him by a gentle lady, an entire
stranger, who had found the joy in believing described to her by the old harper,
and who was eager for others to find it
also.   The thoughtfulness induced by this
question led to his conversion, and dedication to the Christian ministry.

Soon after graduating from Didsbury
Theological Seminary in England he came
to the United States, where he joined the
New England Conference of the Methodist
Episcopal Church.   During his pastorates
he devoted much of his study to the condition of the heathen world, preaching missionary sermons, and publishing articles
on the subject in the church periodicals.
After a few years the project of a mission
in India was taken up by the missionary

Board of the Methodist Episcopal Church,
and appeals were issued to the ministry
for some one to offer himself to go and
begin the work; but for more than three
years no one fitted for the position was
found. Mr. Butler shared the anxiety of
the secretaries and bishops lest the enterprise should fail for want of a suitable
leader. On account of his four young
children he hesitated to offer himself; but
finally his sense of the great need of the
people of India led him to consult with
the authorities, and soon he was appointed
superintendent of the new mission. His
wife bravely seconded him in his determination; and, leaving two boys at school,
they sailed for India in 1856.

On their way they stopped in London to
confer with the secretaries of the different
missionary societies as to the most desirable field for the Methodist Church to
enter where no other agency was at work.
On reaching Calcutta, the same inquiries
were made as to the most needy provinces;
and Oudh and Rohilcund, in the Gangetic

valley, with their twenty millions of souls, were selected as the field of the new mission. The people were intensely hostile to Christianity; and the feeling of unrest in the native army culminated in the dreadful atrocities of the Sepoy Rebellion, only ten weeks after Dr. and Mrs. Butler had begun their work in Bareilly. They were compelled to fly to the mountains, where at Naini Tal they found a refuge for the weary months of anxiety and danger. Their nearest missionary neighbors, of the Presbyterian mission, on the other side of the Ganges, who had fled from Futtyghur for safety, were cruelly massacred, Dr. Butler's home was burned, and a gallows erected for him in the public square at Bareilly, the rebel leader there expressing his great disappointment when he found that the missionary had escaped. The first Eurasian assistant, a young lady, was killed; and the native preacher Joel, who, with his wife, had been spared by the Presbyterian missionaries to aid in beginning the mission, escaped only after enduring many perils.

The church at home believed that Dr. and Mrs. Butler had perished, as no tidings of their safety could reach the outside world; and an obituary was published, so certain did it seem that they had suffered with the many scores of Christian people who fell in that terrible uprising of Moslem hate and heathen superstition. Dr. Butler's first and only experience in handling firearms was at this time, when he and eighty-six Englishmen held the pass up to their place of refuge against the three thousand Sepoys who were sent to capture them. The history of this trying time has been graphically told by Dr. Butler in his "Land of the Veda."

As soon as peace was restored, the work was begun again, with large re-enforcements from the United States. The principal towns of the two provinces were supplied with foreign missionaries, and from these centres the work was pushed out into the villages round about. Earnest street preaching, the distribution of the Scriptures, and hundreds of little schools, were the methods of seed-sowing which in due time have brought forth an abundant harvest.

From the first, Dr. Butler's plan for the missions was to avoid controversy, but to preach Christ as a Saviour for all who will accept him. The first convert from Mohammedanism in this mission was won by this holding up of the cross of Christ to the view of sin-sick souls. He was in the crowd which gathered around the missionary as he stood and preached in the bazaar, and told in simple language what God had done for him in forgiving his sins for Christ's sake. The Mohammedan was greatly moved ; and, seeking the missionary alone, he asked him if he had really experienced this relief from the load of sin of which he had told them in the bazaar. On being assured it was true, he sought and found the same pardon, and became one of the most successful of the native ministers.

The Woman's Foreign Missionary Society came to aid this work with its devoted agents for the special need among the

secluded women in the zenanas. Their
medical work, begun by Dr. Clara Swain
in 1870, the first woman to go as a physician to the women of the East, has accomplished wonders in breaking down the
barriers raised against Christianity. The
work of the Methodist Church now ex-
tends all over India, and before the close
of its forty years of existence counts eighty
thousand members who have been brought
to Christ, with many thousands more
under its instruction and influence.

After ten years of service, Dr. Butler
returned to the United States in broken
health, coming by sailing-vessel around
the Cape of Good Hope during the closing
days of our Civil War. His description of
their anxiety during the four weary months
on board that passed without any news
from the scene of conflict, and of the
tremendous effect of the statements made
by the pilot as he came on board off the
coast of England and announced that the
war was over, the Union saved, and that
the great Lincoln had fallen, is not one of

the least of thrilling tales that Dr. Butler relates in his lectures.

In 1870 he was appointed secretary of the American and Foreign Christian Union, which had as its especial object evangelical work in the Republic of Mexico, just then opening to Protestant influences. This continued till 1873, when some of the churches began to feel that more could be done through separate missions of each denomination; and Dr. Butler was asked to go to Mexico, to establish the work there as he had done in India. Entering the republic soon after the troublous times which ended the so-called Empire of Maximilian of Austria, he found religious liberty in the constitution of the land, though it was as yet imperfectly understood by the masses. Threats of violence were frequently made by the fanatical part of the population, and many times the missionaries' lives were imperilled; but the law has upheld the right of religious liberty, and only one foreigner has lost his life, though many of the Mexicans have suffered bitter persecution and death. In six years the mission was firmly established; and Dr. Butler returned home in shattered health, but soon recovered sufficiently to go up and down throughout the Methodist Church, urging the claims of the missionary work with an eloquence and enthusiasm well nigh irresistible, thus greatly aiding the devoted missionary secretaries in bringing up the contributions of the churches to a more generous figure.

It is a very unusual thing for a missionary to be given the privilege of seeing, after many days, the harvest from the seed he had planted, and another had watered, and to which God had given a wonderful increase. That joy is reserved for the most of the servants of God until the " Well done!" of the Master opens up the eternal bliss of heaven. For Dr. and Mrs. Butler this happy experience began in this life, when in 1883 they went back to India to review the progress of the work. Landing in Bombay, they were welcomed by large congregations of native Christian people; and at every principal station throughout the empire loyal greeting was given to those who came alone, only about thirty years before, with no Christian to stand with them amidst the millions of idolaters and followers of Islam. Now they were received by thousands of native members, who sang, "The morning light is breaking, the darkness disappears," as they welcomed "the Father and Mother of the Mission," with a rejoicing that was a foretaste of the joy of the home-coming in the better land. Truly the little one had become thousands, and darkness and superstition are being put to flight.

Perhaps the most affecting sight of this happy journey was at Chandausi camp-meeting, where Dr. Butler arrived somewhat unexpectedly at the large tent where about eight hundred native Christians were gathered for an early morning service. Joel, the native helper, who had been a faithful minister since the beginning of the mission, was leading the congregation in prayer. It seemed as if Dr. Butler could hardly restrain himself until the petition was finished, when he stepped forward and placed his hands on the shoulders of his beloved fellow-laborer, whose now sightless eyes could not look upon his face, but whose heart recognized the loving touch of his old superintendent. In a moment they were clasped in each other's arms, while the audience rose and sang, as the tears rolled down their cheeks in sympathy with the joy they beheld, "Praise God from whom all blessings flow." No wonder that one of our missionary secretaries should say, "I would rather found a mission than an empire"!

After an extended tour through the various missions, Dr. Butler returned to plead with still greater fervor for this blessed work. His account of the wonderful successes crowning the efforts to evangelize that great people was again an inspiration to the whole Methodist Church. In 1887 he went to revisit Mexico, where he found the work equally full of promise, even if not yet realizing the results of years of labor as fully as the older and larger mission of India. There among the faithful workers was his son, one of the lads who had been so reluctantly left behind when he first went to India, now devoting his life to the redemption of Mexico. Liberty of opinion had gained favor among the people of our sister republic; and the idea of a heart religion, rather than a mere change of form, had become more apparent to the converts. The noble President of Mexico, General Porfirio Diaz, has afforded every protection to Protestant work that the constitution provides; and peace throughout the land has given opportunity for preaching the gospel to the thousands who eagerly hear. In the volume, " Mexico in Transition," written since this visit, Dr. Butler traces the hand of God working in the marvellous events of the history of Mexico that have brought the republic to its present state of freedom and prosperity.

This " veteran missionary of two continents" is passing his declining days in

Newton Centre, Mass., and though in very feeble health, finds great joy in reading the reports which reach him weekly of the glorious victories in the fields which lie so near his heart. By his pen he still pleads for the missions of the church, his latest effort being to secure chapels for the village Christians in India. He is no pessimist, but glows with enthusiasm as he recounts what God has wrought during the present century of missionary effort, and of the manifold agencies of good now being exerted by all branches of the Christian church. He says that God has fulfilled his promise of the "hundred-fold in this life," and he doubts not of the fulfilment of glorious promise of life eternal.

XV.

ADONIRAM JUDSON.

Missionary to Burmah.

Born Aug. 9, 1788; Died April 12, 1850.

ADONIRAM JUDSON.

XV.

ADONIRAM JUDSON.

As Carey was the father of modern missions, Judson was the father of American missions. The thought was no doubt in many minds, and in that circle of young men from which sprung the American Board, each no doubt owed much to the others; but partly from his own strong gifts of body, mind, and downright moral consistency, Judson was the first to carry out in actual missionary life what to others was a plan, a hope, a prayer.

Born Aug. 9, 1788, eldest son of the Congregational minister at Malden, Mass., he could read when three years old, was acute with figures when ten, and, proud and ambitious, entered Brown University, where at nineteen he graduated first in his class. His college course won only praise; but his brightness brought him under the influence of a sceptical college friend, and he came home to declare himself to his father, with characteristic downrightness, an infidel. His father was then minister at Plymouth; and there the son taught school for a year, at this time publishing a school grammar and an arithmetic. He had some thoughts of dramatic writing, and made a tour of travel as far as New York, for a time travelling with a theatrical company.

Returning to Sheffield, Mass., where his uncle was minister, he arranged for a farther journey westward; but was much impressed by a young minister who preached there by exchange; and next day, setting out, took lodging at a country inn, where a young man lay very ill in the adjoining room. Judson was restless, thinking of this man, sick and away from home; and next morning learned with deep feeling that he had died; and, hearing his name, was overwhelmed to find that it was his sceptical college friend. His scheme of travel seemed now impossible; his infidel theories melted away; and he turned his horse's head toward Plymouth, and next month entered an advanced class at Andover Theological Seminary. He joined his father's church in Plymouth the next May.

In the seminary he read Buchanan's "Star in the East," and Syme's "Empire of Ava," and became associated with Samuel Nott, and Samuel J. Mills, Gordon Hall, and others of the Williams College "Haystack" company; and though offered a tutorship at Brown University, and an associate pastorate with Dr. Griffin in Boston, he devoted himself to foreign missionary work.

He had already written to the London Missionary Society; and, after consultation with the teachers and ministers near Andover, he joined his fellow-students in a letter to the Massachusetts General Association of Congregational Churches, which met at Bradford, June 29, 1810, asking advice and help towards missionary service.

This letter was signed by Judson, Nott, Mills, and Samuel Newell.

There had been in existence since 1799 the Massachusetts Missionary Society, organized to carry the gospel to the Indians, and to cultivate the missionary spirit ; but the General Association now organized the American Board of Commissioners for Foreign Missions, and commended the young men to its direction.

Judson was first sent to London to ask the co-operation of the London Society. His ship was captured by a French privateer, and he was imprisoned on ship and in France; but escaped to London, where he was cordially received; but later it was thought best to send him abroad without English assistance.   He was married Feb. 5, 1812, to Miss Ann Hasseltine, daughter of the minister at Bradford ; Feb. 6 he was ordained, and on Feb. 19 he sailed with his bride from Salem for Calcutta.

On the long voyage he became convinced that the Baptist doctrine was in agree-

ment with the Scripture; and after reaching Calcutta he applied to the English
Baptist missionaries at Serampore, and,
with his wife, was immersed, and resigned
his connection with the American Board.

The East India Company presently
ordered him and his fellow American missionaries to return home, subsequently
allowing them to go to Mauritius. There
Mrs. Newell died; and Mr. Rice, who had
also become a Baptist, went to America
to urge the organizing of a Baptist Missionary Society. Judson and his wife, after
four months in Mauritius, largely spent in
mission-work with English soldiers, sailed
for Madras, hoping to establish a mission
at Pulo-Penang, in the Strait of Malacca.
But the only ship sailing in that direction
took them to Rangoon in Burmah, beyond
the protection of the British flag, where
they arrived July 13, 1813. There a son
of Dr. Carey had occupied the English
Baptist mission-house; but he was absent,
and soon afterwards resigned the mission
in their favor.

Burmah was then an independent empire, with a population of about eight millions; the government an absolute despotism, arbitrary and most cruel; the religion Buddhism. Rangoon, near the mouth of the Irrawaddy, is the natural depot of much of Central Asia, and was a strategic centre for Christian missions. It was then a dirty town of about ten thousand inhabitants, intersected by muddy inlets, which filled at high tide. Here Judson began his permanent work.

Two languages were to learn — the common Burmese, and the sacred Pali. The younger Carey had not preached, but had partly made a grammar and dictionary; and Judson at once began his translation of the Bible, which he finished in 1834.

In 1815 Mrs. Judson had to go to Madras for medical advice. That year their first child was born, a little boy who died in infancy. In 1816 Judson seemed breaking down, and hurriedly collected the notes he had made for a Burman grammar. It was published twenty years later, and greatly praised for comprehensive and concise accuracy. Partially recovering, he imported a printing-press from Serampore and a printer from America, and published his " View of the Christian Religion," the first of a series of tracts that had a strong influence with that thoughtful and reading people. Mrs. Judson also published a catechism.

These publications were followed by the appearance of *Inquirers*, the first one coming March 7, 1817, and marking an epoch in the work.

With a deepened sense of the need of evangelistic work, Judson now went to Chittagong to find some native Christian who could preach and teach in Burmese. He was unexpectedly detained there seven months, during which his wife, with some missionary helpers who had joined them, maintained the work under vexatious persecutions, displaying great endurance and wonderful skill and diplomacy with the native authorities ; and later going through the trials of an epidemic of cholera. On his return Judson built an open *zayat*, a shed of bamboo, for public evangelization, with a room for assemblies of worship, and another, opening on the garden, for women's classes. The *zayat* was on a main public thoroughfare, under the shadow of the chief pagoda. Here he conversed with men of different classes, some of profound Oriental learning, and saw how the scepticism of European philosophy has been anticipated in the subtler scepticisms of India, which have undermined Oriental faith, and made preparation for a faith more rational.

The first regular service was held in the *zayat* April 4, 1819, Judson having been in Rangoon nearly six years, and then first venturing to preach in the native tongue. The 27th of the following June he baptized his first Burman convert, Moung Nau.

In November there were rumors of persecutions, and public services were suspended for several Sundays, and two new converts were baptized privately; and greater interest bringing new threats from the authorities, Judson went to Ava, the capital, to lay the matter before the king. The journey and return consumed over two months, and seemed rather to produce more explicit threats ; and Judson resolved to remove to Chittagong, under British rule.

But now the little circle of converts awoke to independent life and courage. They could not bear to be scattered, but begged that, if the missionaries must go, it would not be till their membership was increased to ten, and they organized under some leader to hold them together and help their Christian life. Departure was therefore postponed ; and ten months later the tenth convert and first woman was received into the church. This was on the eve of Judson's sailing to Calcutta with his wife because of her ill heath ; and through this absence the little church stood steadfast even under persecution.

Then the persecution ceased. A girls' school was opened ; and the work took so interesting a form that, though Mrs. Judson's health compelled her to go to America, her husband remained at Rangoon.

He was now joined by Dr. Price, a medical missionary, whose remarkable success, especially in operations for cataract, led to his being summoned to Ava, to the king; and here Judson thought it best to accompany him.

This movement brought the whole missionary work at once under favorable notice of the court. There was no more talk of persecution, but apparently the largest opening for greatly enlarged work. Judson came into the presence of the king, and received the royal invitation to transfer his work from Rangoon to the capital; and after Mrs. Judson's return from America with improved health, and with re-enforcements for Rangoon, they removed to Ava, arriving there in January, 1824.

The court favor at Ava, however, was clouded over by a change of ministers, almost before their actual arrival. Many postponements and hindrances impeded their work, in spite of the favor held by Dr. Price's medical reputation; and in a few months the outbreak of war between

Burmah and England threw the mission into confusion and dismay. There was a general suspicion of all persons of English speech; and ere long Judson, Dr. Price, and five others were arrested and thrown into prison.

This imprisonment lasted for eleven months in the "death-prison" at Ava, and afterwards for six months in the country prison of Oung-peu-la. Mrs. Judson was not arrested, though her house was searched and all valuable property confiscated. She made almost daily visits to the prison, though often refused admittance, and also to the palace, maintaining the respect and friendship of some of the court, and was able to carry her husband food and clothing, and after some months to build him a little bamboo shed in the prison yard, where he could sometimes be by himself, and where at times she was allowed to be with him. In January, 1825, a little daughter was born to her; and a few months later she went through an epidemic of small-pox.

The horrors of Judson's imprisonment can only be imagined; crowded into narrow quarters with over a hundred common criminals, loaded with fetters, at first three pairs of fetters, afterwards five pairs, with no conveniences for cleanliness or even decency. After eleven months the captives were suddenly removed from the city prison, and with agonizingly painful marching taken to the country prison of Oung-peu-la. There, after days of weariness and pain, at night, for security, a bamboo pole was passed between the fettered ankles of a string of prisoners, and then hoisted by ropes till their shoulders only rested on the floor. Daily and nightly torture, racking fever, half starvation, and daily anticipation of death, marked these terrible months.

But the success of the British arms at length compelled the king to send Judson and Dr. Price as interpreting envoys to negotiate peace; and the British commander made his first absolute demand the release of the missionaries, and the Judsons returned to Rangoon. During his impris-

onment his unfinished manuscript translation of the Bible was hid by his wife in a
cotton pillow on which he slept. This was
thrown aside as worthless when his prison
was changed, but was found and saved by
a native convert.

The Rangoon church being scattered, a
new mission was begun at Amherst on
British territory, but later removed to
Maulmain, a more important centre. This
greatly prospered, though they had no more
their youthful strength; and during Judson's
absence at Ava, attempting to secure religious toleration, his wife died of a fever,
and he returned soon to lay their little child
by her side.

With broken heart and health he became
almost wildly ascetic; living much alone,
fasting and praying whole days in the
woods. He relinquished part of his slen-
der missionary pay, and made over to the
Board about six thousand dollars, including presents and fees from the British
government for treaty-negotiation service,
and some private means brought origi-

nally from home. In 1830 he again attempted to penetrate Burmah, living six months at Prome, half-way between Rangoon and Ava, but was driven back by Burman intrigues. He then began a work among the wild Karens of the jungle, and with great success.

In 1834 he married Mrs. Sarah Boardman, widow of a fellow missionary. He completed his Bible, pronounced by Dr. Wayland the best translation in India, and by Orientalists " a perfect literary work."

In 1845 his health and his wife's was so broken that they sailed for Mauritius, and from there for America; but she died Sept. 1, while in port at St. Helena. Judson, with three children, reached Boston on Oct. 15.

He was in America till July, 1846, and, before re-embarking for India, was married to Miss Emily Chubbuck, who was known as a writer under the name of Fanny Forester.

His last years, 1846–1850, were spent in another earnest but unsuccessful attempt to break through Burman bigotry, in the continuation of his Burman dictionary and other literary work, and in the forwarding of the general missionary enterprise.

Towards the end of 1849 his health declined alarmingly. His sixty years had contained more wear and strain than come to many a long life. The " keen sword had worn out the scabbard." In the spring of 1850 it was hoped that a sea voyage might help him ; and he was carried on shipboard April 8, but died April 12, and was buried at sea.

The late Rev. A. J. Gordon, D.D., in writing of the illustrious missionary whose name he bears, says : " Park Street Church in Boston, whose call the Spirit constrained Judson to decline seventy-five years ago, is still a large body, numbering perhaps a thousand members ; but the church in Burmah, which that same Spirit led Judson to found, numbers to-day thirty thousand communicants, with a great company beside who have fallen asleep."

XVI.

JOHN G. PATON.

Missionary to the New Hebrides.

Born May 24, 1824.

JOHN G. PATON.

XVI.

JOHN G. PATON.

John Gibson Paton was born May 24, 1824, near Dumfries, in the south of Scotland. His father was a stocking-maker; and although his family was little blessed in this world's goods, it was devoutly religious. When young John had reached his fifth year, the family moved to a new home in the ancient village of Torthorwald.

Their new home was of the usual thatched cottage, plainly but substantially built. It was one-story, and was divided into three rooms. One end room served as the living-room of the family, the other as a shop, and the middle one was the family sanctuary. To the sanctuary the father retired after each meal to offer up prayer in behalf of his family. Paton himself says : " We occasionally heard the pa-

thetic echoes of a trembling voice, pleading
as if for life ; and we learned to slip out and
in past that door on tiptoe, not to disturb
that holy colloquy." Is it strange that from
this family there should come three ministers of the gospel ?

In early boyhood John was sent to the
parish school, presided over by a man
named Smith, who, although of high scholarship, was often unreasonable when in a
rage. At one time his temper got the
best of him, and he unjustly punished
Paton, who ran home. Returning at his
mother's entreaty, he was again abused,
and left the school never to return. He
now began to learn his father's trade, making an effort at the same time to keep up
his studies. The work was hard, and he
toiled from six in the morning until ten at
night. At this time he learned much in a
mechanical line which was of use to him
later in the missionary field. He saved
enough money from his wages to enable
him to attend Dumfries Academy for six
weeks. As a result of his earnest endeavor

to keep up his studies since leaving the parish school, he was able now as a young man to obtain a position as district visitor and tract distributer of the West Campbell Street Reformed Presbyterian Church in Glasgow, with the privilege of attending the Free Church Normal Seminary. There were two applicants for the position; and as the trustees could not decide between them, they offered to let them work together and divide the salary, which was £50 a year.

Paton's health failed him, and he returned home. After recovering fully he returned to Glasgow, where he had a hard struggle with poverty. At one time, having no money, he secured a place as teacher of the Mary Hill Free School. This school had a bad reputation, many teachers having been forced to leave it because of trouble with the scholars. Paton managed by force of kindness to make friends of all the pupils; and when he finally left, the school was in a more prosperous condition than it had ever been before.

After leaving the school, he took a position as a worker in the Glasgow city mission. In this work he was remarkably successful. For ten years he was engaged in these labors, keeping up the study of theology all the time. Then, hearing that a helper was wanted to join the Rev. John Inglis in the New Hebrides, he offered himself and was accepted. This step was distasteful to many, who insisted that there were heathen enough at home; but, as Paton says, those who spoke thus invariably neglected the home heathen themselves. On the 16th of April, 1858, Mr. and Mrs. Paton set sail from Scotland in the Clutha for New Hebrides.

They stopped a few days at Melbourne, and from there sailed for Aneityum, the most southern of the New Hebrides. In twelve days they arrived off Aneityum; but the captain, a profane and hard-hearted man, refused to land them, and the landing was made with great difficulty, with the help of Dr. Geddie, in mission boats. They decided to settle on the eastern shore of Tanna, a small island a few miles north of Aneityum, which was inhabited by ferocious savages. Mr. and Mrs. Mathieson, co-laborers with them, settled on the northwestern shore of the same island.

The natives on Tanna were sunk to the lowest depths of heathenism, going about with no covering save an apron and paint — having no ideas of right or wrong, worshipping and fearing numerous gods, living in a continual dread of evil spirits, constantly fighting among themselves, and always eating the bodies of the slain — such were the creatures whom Paton and his wife hoped to bring to a knowledge of the gospel.

They landed on Tanna the 5th of November, 1858. On the 15th of February, 1859, a child was born to them. Mrs. Paton's health from this time on was very feeble, and on March 3d she died of a sudden attack of pneumonia. Unaided and alone, the bereaved husband buried his beloved wife. Over her body he placed a mound of stones, making it as attractive as he could, and then with a heavy heart

turned to his work.   Soon after the child,
a boy, followed the mother.   These two
sorrows came as a terrible blow to Paton,
and for some time he was prostrated.   He
rallied, however, and began to work hard
and steadily to enlighten those poor savages, who upon every occasion robbed and
abused him.

Mr. Paton, writing of this period, says:
" On beholding these natives in their paint
and nakedness and misery, my heart was
as full of horror as of pity.   Had I given
up my much-beloved work and my dear
people in Glasgow, with so many delightful associates, to consecrate my life to these
degraded creatures?   Was it possible to
teach them right and wrong, to Christianize
or even to civilize them?   But that was
only a passing feeling.   I soon got as
deeply interested in them, and all that
tended to advance them, and to lead them
to the knowledge of Jesus, as ever I had
been in my work in Glasgow."

The greatest opposition to his work was
occasioned by the godless traders on the

island, who caused more trouble than did the natives themselves. These traders did not relish the idea of the natives being taught the gospel, for they feared to lose their influence over them. They incited the different tribes to fight with each other, and then sold arms to the contestants. They stirred up bad feeling against the missionaries, and urged the natives to either kill or drive them away.

From the time he landed until he left Tanna, Paton was in continual danger of losing his life. Again and again armed bands came to his house at night to kill him. He himself said that he knew of fifty times when his life was in imminent danger, and his escape was due solely to the grace of God. Only once did he resort to force, or rather the appearance of force. A cannibal entered his house, and would have killed him, had he not raised an empty pistol, at sight of which the cowardly fellow fled.

The feeling toward him became so hostile that he was obliged at last to leave his house, and take refuge in the village of a friendly chief named Nowar. Here he prepared to leave that part of the island, and sail around to Mr. Mathieson's station. He secured a canoe, but when he went to launch it he found there were no paddles. After he had managed to get these, the chief Arkurat refused to let him go. Having prevailed upon the vacillating savage to consent, he finally sailed away with his three native helpers and a boy. The wind and waves, however, forced them to put back, and after five hours of hard rowing they returned to the spot they had left. The only way left now was to walk overland. He got a friendly native to show him the path, and after escaping death most miraculously on the way, arrived at Mr. Mathieson's. Here they were still persecuted. At one time the mission buildings were fired, but a tornado which suddenly came up extinguished the flames. On the day following, the ship which had been sent to rescue them arrived and they embarked. Thus Paton had to abandon his work on Tanna, after toiling there over three years.

For a time he sought needed rest and change in Australia, where he presented the cause of missions to the churches. On many occasions he came into contact with the aborigines of that continent, and on every occasion his love for missionary work was exhibited. At one time, when a crowd of savages crazed with rum were fighting among themselves, he went among them, and by his quiet and persistent coaxing, managed to get them all to lie down and sleep off the effects of the spirits.

From Australia, Paton went to Scotland. He travelled all over the country, speaking in behalf of the mission. While in Scotland he married Margaret Whitecross, a woman well fitted to be the wife and helper of such a man. Leaving Scotland in the latter part of 1864, they arrived in the New Hebrides in the early part of 1865.

In 1866 they settled on Aniwa, an

island near Tanna. The old Tannese chief, Nowar, who had always been friendly to Paton, was very anxious to have him settle on Tanna. Seeing that this was impossible, Nowar took from his arm the white shells, insignia of chieftainship, and binding them to the arm of a visiting Aniwan chief, said: "By these you promise to protect my missionary and his wife and child on Aniwa. Let no evil befall them, or by this pledge I and my people will avenge it." This act of the old chief did much to insure the future safety of Paton and his family.

Aniwa is a small island, only nine miles long by three and one-half wide. There is a scarcity of rain, but the heavy dews and moist atmosphere keep the land covered with verdure. The natives were like those on Tanna, although they spoke a different language.

They were well received by the natives, who escorted them to their temporary abode, and watched them at their meals. The first duty was to build a house. An elevated site was purchased, where it was afterward learned all the bones and refuse of the Aniwan cannibal feast, for years, had been buried. The natives probably thought that, when they disturbed these, the missionary and his helpers would drop dead. In building the house, an incident occurred which afterward proved of great benefit to Paton. One day, having need of some nails and tools, he picked up a chip and wrote a few words on it. Handing it to an old chief, he told him to take it to Mrs. Paton. When the chief saw her look at the chip and then get the things needed, he was filled with amazement. From that time on he took great interest in the work of the mission, and when the Bible was being translated into the Aniwa language he rendered invaluable aid.

Another chief, with his two sons, visited the mission-house and was much interested ; but when they were returning home, one of his sons became very ill. Of course he thought the missionary was to blame, and threatened to kill the latter; but when, by the use of proper medicine, Paton brought the boy back to health again, the chief went to the opposite extreme, and was ever afterward a most devoted helper.

The first convert on Aniwa was the chief Mamokei. He often came to drink tea with the missionary family, and afterward brought with him chief Naswai and his wife; and all three were soon converted. Mamokei brought his little daughter to be educated in the mission. Many orphan children were also put under their care, and often these little children warned them of plots against their lives.

In the early part of the work on Aniwa, an incident happened which was amusing as well as romantic. A young Aniwan was in love with a young widow, living in an island village. Unfortunately, there were thirty other young men who also were suitors; and as the one who married her would probably be killed by the others, none dared to venture. After consulting

with Paton, the young man went to her
village at night and stole away with her.
The others were furious, but were pacified
by Paton, who made them believe she
was not worth troubling themselves over.
After three weeks had passed, the young
man came out of hiding, and asked permission to bring her to the mission-house,
which was granted. The next day she
appeared in time for services. As the dis-
tinguishing feature of a Christian on Aniwa is that he wears more clothing than
the heathen native, and as this young lady
wished to show very plainly in what direction her sympathies extended, she appeared
on the scene clad in a variety and abun-
dance of clothing which it would be hard to
equal. It was mostly European, at least.
Over her native grass skirt she wore a
man's drab-colored great-coat, sweeping
over her heels. Over this was a vest, and
on her head was a pair of trousers, one
leg trailing over each shoulder. On one
shoulder, also, was a red shirt, on the
other a striped one; and, last of all, a

red shirt was twisted around her head as
a turban.

Many stories might be told illustrating
the results of the early efforts of the missionary, but we pass on to that of the sinking of the well.   As has already been said,
there is little rain on Aniwa.   The juice of
the cocoanut is largely used by the natives
in place of drinking-water.   Paton resolved
to sink a well, much to the astonishment
of the natives, who, when he explained his
plan to them, thought him crazy.   He began to dig; and the friendly old chief kept
men near him all the time, for fear he
would take his own life, for they thought
surely he must have gone mad.   He managed to get some of the natives to help him,
paying them in fish-hooks; but when the
depth of twelve feet was reached the sides
of the excavation caved in, and after that
no native would enter it.   Paton then constructed a derrick; and they finally consented to help pull up the loaded pails,
while he dug.   Day after day he toiled,
till the hole was thirty feet deep.   Still no

water was found. That day he said to the old chief, " I think Jehovah God will give us water to-morrow from that hole." But the chief said they expected to see him fall through into the sea. Next morning he sunk a small hole in the bottom of the well, and from this hole there spurted a stream of water. Filling the jug with the water, he passed it round to the natives, telling them to examine and taste it. They were so awe-stricken that not one dared look over the edge into the well. At last they formed a line, holding each other by the hand, and first one looked over, then the next, etc., till all had seen the water in the well. When they were told that they all could use the water from that well, the old chief exclaimed, " Missi, what can we do to help you now?" He directed them to bring coral rock to line the well with, which they did with a will. That was the beginning of a new era on Aniwa. The following Sunday the chief preached a sermon on the well. In the days that followed multitudes of natives brought their idols to the mission, where they were destroyed. Henceforth Christianity gained a permanent foothold on the island.

In 1869 the first communion was held, twelve out of twenty applicants being admitted to the church. In speaking of his emotions during the first communion, Paton says, " I shall never taste a deeper bliss until I gaze on the glorified face of Jesus himself."

In 1884 he returned to Scotland, his main object being to secure £6,000 for a mission-ship. He addressed many assemblages of different kinds, and succeeded in getting not only the £6,000 required, but £3,000 beside. He returned to Aniwa in 1886, and continued his work.

Recently he again visited England, and also the United States. He is now back on Aniwa — Aniwa, no longer a savage island, but by the grace of God a Christian land. There he expects to remain till summoned to his reward before the heavenly throne.

In this sketch an attempt has been made

to give only a brief account of the work of this great missionary. No adequate idea can be given of his untiring zeal, his forgetfulness of self, and his simple faith in God. It is probable that no one has ever visited America in the interest of foreign missions who has made so deep an impression of the triumphs of the gospel among vicious and degraded peoples as has the eminent missionary hero, John G. Paton.

XVII.

ALEXANDER M. MACKAY.

Missionary to Uganda.

Born Oct. 13, 1849; Died Feb. 8, 1890.

XVII.

ALEXANDER M. MACKAY.

GREEK and Roman, Arab, Turk, and
Christian pioneer, at various times, and ac-
tuated by different purposes, have wended
their ways into the unknown land of the
Dark Continent; and Africa for ages has
been the scene of thrilling adventure, perilous labor, and sublime life-sacrifice.

Livingstone, Speke, Gordon, Stanley,
Hannington, and others, are numbered
among the world's heroes; and conspicuous upon this roll of noble men must now
be written the name of Alexander M.
Mackay.

Born Oct. 13, 1849, in the little village
of Rhynie, Aberdeen County, Scotland, in
his father's home, — the Free Church
Manse, — Mr. Mackay was at once blessed
with a godly upbringing in the midst of

intellectual surroundings. Mr. Mackay's father was a man of great literary ability, and for fourteen years carefully carried on the daily instruction of his boy. At three years of age Alexander Mackay read the New Testament with ease, and at seven his text-books were Milton's " Paradise Lost," Russell's " History of Modern Europe," Gibbon's " Decline and Fall of the Roman Empire," and Robertson's " History of the Discovery of America."

He was his father's constant companion in his walks; and stories are now told of the villagers' wonder at seeing the boy often " stop to look for something in the road; " while from point of fact he was watching his father's stick trace the supposed course of the Zambesi River, or outline the demonstrating of a proposition in Euclid. Letters were frequently received at the Manse from Hugh Miller, Sir Roderick Murchison, and other eminent scholars, all of which were read and talked about in the family circle; and in these ways the boy's mind rapidly developed.

At ten years of age he had great skill in map-making, and wonderful dexterity in type-setting ; and very accurate were the proof-sheets turned out from his little printing-press.

In 1864 he entered the grammar school at Aberdeen, and here he worked well; he seldom joined the excursions of the young people, but preferred to become initiated in art photography, or to watch the workmen in the great shipyards. And thus from different sources practical knowledge of many things was by him early acquired.

In 1865 Mackay sustained a great loss in the death of his mother, whose parting injunction, to " Search the Scriptures," became a duty, always continued. In the fall of 1867 Mackay entered the Free Church Training School for Teachers, in Edinburgh ; and there he won the admiration of pupils and teachers by his scholarly ability for two years, and then entered the Edinburgh University for a three years' course in classics, applied mechanics, higher mathematics, and natural philosophy, fol-

lowed by a year's study of surveying and for-
tification with Lieutenant Mackie, Professor
of Engineering.   For two years (1870–
72), while Secretary of the Engineering Society, and tutor each morning at George
Watson's College, Mackay daily took the
tram-car to Leith, and spent his afternoons
in model-making, and in turning, fitting,
and erecting machinery in the engineering
works of Messrs. Miller and Herbert.   His
evenings were employed in attending lectures on chemistry and geology at the
School of Arts and other places.   Sundays
he gave to regular attendance at religious
services, and to teaching in Dr. Guthrie's
Original Ragged School.

In November, 1873, Mackay went to Germany to study the language, and at once
secured a good position as draughtsman in
the Berlin Union Engineering Co.   While
thus employed, he spent his evenings in
translating Lübsen's " Differential and In-
tegral Calculus," and in inventing an agricultural machine, which obtained the first
prize at the exhibition of steam-engines

held at Breslau. The directors of the company, recognizin Mackay's ability, soon made him chief of the locomotive department.

In May, 1874, Mackay became a boarding member in the family of Herr Hofprediger Baur, one of the ministers at the cathedral, and one of the chaplains; and in this cultured and pious home Mackay derived many advantages, and met once a week at the Bible readings, the *élite* of the Christian society of Berlin, among whom were Gräfin von Arnim, sister of Prince Bismarck, and Graf and Gräfin Egloffstein,who gave great interest to Mackay's later labors.

At this time Herr Hofprediger Baur was actively engaged in a German translation of the life of Bishop Patteson; and this work, together with the Professor's sympathy, proved a stimulus to the decision Mackay had already made to devote his life to missionary work; this decision having been arrived at after reading his sister's account of Dr. Burns Thompson's urgent appeal to young men to go to Madagascar. With Mackay to decide was to act; but as he could not at once enter the field as clergyman or doctor, he determined to do so as engineering missionary (a most practical and far-sighted determination); and, blessed with his father's sanction, he offered his services to the London Missionary Society, but was answered that Madagascar "was not yet ripe for his assistance." At this time Mackay received an offer of partnership in a large engineering firm in Moscow, which without hesitation he refused, believing an opening for him in mission-work would soon be found.

In 1875 the *Daily Telegraph* published Stanley's famous letter " challenging Christendom to send missionaries to Uganda; " and the Church Missionary Society gladly accepted Mackay's offer of service in their future mission to the Victoria Nyanza. Early in March, Mackay returned to England; and in the development of plans the Church Missionary Society determined to combine the industrial with the religious

element, and sanctioned the purchase of a
light cedar boat for navigation, and also
appropriated three hundred pounds for a
portable engine and boiler to be fitted into
a wooden boat to be built by the missionaries on the Nyanza. Many weary days
Mackay gave to finding, in London, an
engineer who would build an engine on
the principle of welded rings, each light
enough to be transported by two men.
But finally an engine after his own design
was built, and tools of all kinds were ready
for the enterprise ; and on the 27th of
April, 1876, in a company of eight, Mackay
left England in the Peshawur, and arrived
at Zanzibar May 29.

To facilitate the journey to the great
lake, the mission party intended to sail up
the Wami River, and on the 12th of June
Mackay and Lieutenant Smith started in
the Daisy on a voyage of exploration, but,
after many days of hardship, they found
both the Wami and Kingani Rivers un-
navigable, and were obliged to proceed inland on foot. At Ugogo, in November,

Mackay, who had charge of the third section of the caravan, was taken seriously ill, and was obliged to return to the coast, where he was instructed by the Church Missionary Society to delay starting for the interior until June, 1877. He employed the intervening time in sending a relief caravan to his brethren on the lake, and in cutting a good road to Mpwapa, two hundred and thirty miles inland.

March, 1878, Mackay heard of the murder of Lieutenant Smith and Mr. O'Neill, who had reached the lake months before, and hurried with all speed to the scene of the disaster, the island of Ukerewe, hoping by friendly intervention to prevent further bloodshed.

June 13 he arrived at Kagei, and had his first glimpse of the great lake. With joy he realized that the worst part of his journey was over. Piled together in a hut, Mackay found much of the valuable property conveyed to this point by the first sections of the expedition, and left in charge of the natives. Heaped together lay boiler-shells and books, papers and piston-rods, steam-pipes and stationery, printers' types, saws, and garden-seed, tins of bacon and bags of clothes, portable forges and boiler-fittings, here a cylinder, there its sole plate.

"Ten days' hard work from dawn to dark, and," Mackay wrote, "the engines for our steamer stand complete to the last screw; the boiler is ready to be riveted, tools and types have separate boxes, and rust and dust are thrown out of doors. It seems a miracle that I find almost everything complete, even to its smallest belonging, after a tedious voyage of seven hundred miles." The Daisy, rebuilt by O'Neill, but now greatly damaged, employed Mackay's attention; and setting up his rotary grindstone, to the wonderment of the natives, he patched the sides and calked the seams, and made the boat again seaworthy.

After his great labor in repairs, Mackay, in spite of danger to himself, visited Ukerewe, and with tactful courage held a friendly visit with King Lkonge. After this visit Mackay was a victim of dysentery; but at length, joined by Mr. Wilson, and favored with a good breeze, he sailed in the Daisy for Uganda. Four days of fine sailing, and then they were wrecked; and eight weeks of hard labor was given to making a new boat out of the Daisy.

Mackay finally reached Rubaga, the capital of Uganda, Nov. 6. A friendly interview was at once had with King Mtèsa, who had told Stanley to send the " white men," and for a time affairs at court went smoothly. Mtèsa and his subjects were much interested by accounts of railways, electricity, astronomy, and physiology; and Mackay gained great influence by his mechanical skill, which caused wonder and admiration.

Mtèsa appeared very anxious to hear more about the Christian religion to which Stanley had introduced him, and every Sunday religious services were held at court. From the first, the Arabs who centred in Rubaga were jealous of Mackay, fearing his influence would overthrow the slave traffic, which brought them here as elsewhere in Africa. They used all means to turn Mtèsa against the white man, the most potent of which were the rich presents, including fire-arms, presented to the king.

The Arabs were no more formidable enemies to Mackay than were the Roman Catholic missionaries, who came soon after his arrival, confusing Mtèsa with their claims to the true religion, and instituting a cruel persecution against the Protestants.

In April, 1880, Mackay, finding his store of goods nearly exhausted by the thieving of Mtèsa's chiefs, went to Uyui for supplies, and during this trip barely escaped being murdered by the natives. At this time Mtèsa turned entirely away from the teachings which Mackay and his friends had labored for two years to inculcate, — two years of labor, poverty, danger, and ofttimes threatened starvation, Mackay keeping his comrades alive by the sale of articles made by himself in his workshop.

" Besides teaching his pupils reading,

writing, and arithmetic, Mackay gave them daily lessons " in building and designing. He built a house for the mission party, which was a source of wonder to all, and caused Mtèsa to ask instruction for the natives in wood and iron ; and when Mackay asked a piece of ground to build huts on, he at once gave him twenty acres. To the natives Mackay's most wonderful achievement was a cart painted red and blue, and drawn by oxen.

From time to time Mackay's great work was supplemented by co-laborers sent by the Church Missionary Society ; and in March, 1881, his heart was delighted by the baptism of five converts by Mr. O'Flaherty. Early in 1883 the Rev. E. C. Gordon and Mr. Wise joined Mackay ; in May of the same year the Rev. R. P. Ashe arrived, and the prospects of the Mission were most encouraging until October, 1884, when Mtèsa died.

The king's son, Mwanga, succeeded to the throne — a youth with all his father's vices and none of his virtues ; and a reign

of blood and terror followed, beginning
with the burning of two Christian lads,
who met their death with songs of praise,
and were the first martyrs to the faith in
Uganda. The storm of persecution spent
its full force in October, 1885, when news
reached the king that white men had come
by the Masai route, and were entering
Uganda by the "back door." Orders were
sent to kill the whole party. Prevented
from leaving the court, Ashe and Mackay
awaited in dread suspense, which gave way
to despair, when news of Bishop Hannington's death was confirmed. In the months
that followed, lives of missionaries and converts were in constant danger; still the
gospel spread, and young men came daily
to the mission house for translated copies.

In May, 1886, thirty of the missionaries'
faithful converts were slowly burned alive.
Mackay was now anxious to get out of the
country, but was refused permission to
leave. New missionaries with presents
would have bought his escape; but he
would not write for men to come to

Uganda in the disturbed condition of affairs, so bravely stayed on, even after he had unselfishly obtained leave for Ashe to go.

Alone, weary in soul and body, his life in imminent danger, Mackay worked early and late in translating and printing the Scriptures. News of the Emin Pasha expedition reached the king; and warned by French priests that Stanley and Mackay would put their heads together to "eat the country," Mwanga decided that Mackay must leave Uganda. Arranging that Mr. Gordon should come to care for the converts, who were only comforted by his assurances that he was but going to the south of the lake, Mackay turned away from the country where he had spent nine eventful years, — years of deep experiences, of toils and privations; years that had silvered his hair and calmed the restless impulses of his youth; but his watchword was unchanged — "Africa for Christ."

After much weary wandering, Mackay fell in with a friendly chief in the land of

Usambiro; and here, single-handed and alone, he began the great work of a new mission station. A band of five men, headed by Bishop Parker, and including his old friend and fellow worker, Ashe, soon came to cheer his lonely life. A few happy weeks together — then Bishop Parker and Mr. Blackburn died of fever; Mr. Walker went to Uganda; Mr. Ashe was compelled to return home on account of bad health; Mackay was again alone.

And again this all-round missionary set himself to the work of teaching, translating, printing, binding, doctoring, and building; and in the midst of these many and arduous labors, he found time to give to the world practical suggestions, now being carried out; viz., " Stations all over Uganda," and, " a railway from the coast to the lake."

In September, 1889, Stanley visited Mackay on his return to the coast, and " In Darkest Africa" gives with unstinted praise an account of the mission station, with its clay-built house " garnished with missionary pictures, and shelves filled with choice, useful books, its hospitable table with wholesome food (home-made bread and coffee) ; the mission-school of neat, well-mannered boys, a launch's boiler, and a canoe under construction, saw-pits, and cattle-fold, all the work of " the best missionary since Livingstone."

Stanley and his party urged Mackay to join the homeward expedition, but with characteristic fidelity he refused to leave until some one came to take his place. "European platforms and royal receptions" were never his; but Feb. 8, 1890, his tireless energy rested, and the title-deeds of his labor were recorded, in divine Presence, upon the brow of every converted black in Uganda.

XVIII.

BISHOP WILLIAM TAYLOR,

Missionary in Africa, India, and South America.

BORN MAY 2, 1821.

XVIII.

BISHOP WILLIAM TAYLOR.

JAMES TAYLOR was one of five brothers who emigrated from County Armagh, Ireland, to the colony of Virginia about one hundred and forty years ago, fine specimens of that hardy, energetic race known as Scotch-Irish, of the old Covenanter type. Their names in the order of their birth were, George, James, William, John, and Canfield. They all fought for American freedom in the Revolution of 1776, John being killed, and Canfield a prisoner of war when the new nation was born. George and James both married daughters of Captain Audley Paul, of the same hardy clan, who was a fellow-lieutenant of George Washington, and was present on the morning of " Braddock's defeat," when young Washington ventured to suggest that the In-

dians would have to be fought in their
own fashion.   Audley Paul, with many others, swam the Allegheny ; and the sword
he carried in that disastrous engagement,
and in his years of marching and fighting
as a captain in the War of Independence,
is a relic in the Taylor family.

The Taylors had invested in land and
slaves ; but the Pauls, being religiously
opposed to slavery, so indoctrinated the
rising generation of Taylors, that they
set the slaves free as fast as they came
into their possession by inheritance.   A
younger son of James and Ann Taylor,
Stuart, married Martha E. Hickman, of
an English family that had settled in
Delaware ; and their first-born, William,
came to them in Rockbridge County, Virginia, May 2, 1821. Of the eleven sons
and daughters of which he was the eldest,
the father wrote, on his fiftieth wedding
anniversary : " God has blessed us in our
children. They are all healthy, all religious,
all Methodists, all industrious, all peaceable
and peace-makers ; all married except Re-

becca and John, who are in heaven ; all settled in comfortable homes of their own,
except the three itinerant Methodist ministers. We are happy then to know that our
work is done. Our sun is setting, and not
a cloud in the west. We are waiting cheer-
fully on the bank of the river for the boat-
man to come and take us home."

Before the conversion of his parents,
while still the occupant of the " trundle-
bed," William was deeply convicted of sin.
He had learned to read portions of Scripture concerning the love of Jesus ; and one
day he heard a black girl tell of the testimony of a black collier to his present saving power ; and on this evidence, given
second-hand, he was enabled " to receive
and trust Jesus, and come into blessed
union with God." He early had a desire
to preach the gospel, and daily witnessed
and worked for the salvation of souls.
The occasion of his reception of his first
license as an " exhorter " was immediately
preceded by a dream, prophetic of his life
work. In his dream he was listening to

an earnest preacher of the gospel, who, at the close of the sermon, sang a solo while the larger part of the congregation retired. Then the preacher, looking-steadfastly at him as he sat about twelve feet in front of him, said : "William, I have known for some time that God has a special work for you to do. If you will follow his Spirit, confer not with flesh and blood, turn neither to the right nor to the left, your wisdom will be like the continual dropping into a bucket."

The words but expressed a vision of the whole thing clearly presented to his view, including a large, empty bucket, with the rapid dropping of the clearest, purest water. The following Sunday, after the sermon, about thirty persons remained for class-meeting, the preacher singing a hymn while the rest retired. Coming down from the pulpit he said to him, "William, I want you to go out." He hastened home, wondering why he should be ordered out of the church in the presence of the whole class ; while the pastor said to the people,

" I have had my eye on William Taylor
for some time past, and, believing that
God has a special work for him to do, I
wish to submit his name to the church
as a suitable person to receive an official
license to exhort."

For seven years, from 1842, he was engaged in pioneer preaching in the hills of
Virginia and Maryland, and in the city of
Baltimore. The seven years succeeding,
he was organizing churches in California.
Mr. Taylor was the first Methodist missionary in San Francisco, where he continued his street preaching, and became
popularly known as " Father Taylor." His
desire was to remain there in the pastorate,
but having become personally responsible
for the debts of a church that was burned,
he assumed their payment. In order to
secure money he wrote and sold books.
The next seven years he travelled in the
United States and Canada, usually remaining only three nights in each church,
preaching two nights with " direct soul-
saving results," and lecturing the third

nignt, generally selling from two to three hundred dollars' worth of his books at the altar rail at the close.

In May, 1862, he commenced a foreign evangelizing tour, the principal fields being the Australian Colonies, New Zealand, Tasmania, Cape Colony, Caffraria and Natal, West India Islands, British Guiana, South America, England, Ireland, and Scotland, Ceylon and India. Having labored during the year 1871 in the mission of North India as an evangelist, he opened new fields in South India in 1872, purely on the line of self-support. From the churches organized, not from accretion, but by new creation, consisting of new-born souls, two annual conferences were formed, and the number has since increased to four.

He returned to the United States in 1875, purposing to resume work in South India the following year, but was detained by having to sell more books to procure funds to pay passage of more missionaries, for that rapidly developing work. In all, he has personally sold over two hundred thousand dollars' worth of his own books. In 1878 he was led to open self-supporting missions in South America, and in 1879 he opened the "Transit and Building Fund" to help found self-supporting missions. While in South America he received a request to represent South India Conference, as a lay delegate to the General Conference of 1884, the body that made him missionary Bishop of Africa.

His previous knowledge of this difficult field enabled him to adopt methods at the start that have proved well adapted to its peculiarities. The plan of missionary work well suited to Asiatic countries, with their Oriental type of civilization, comprising school work and gospel preaching, was not broad enough for a purely heathen country like Africa; so to these he added two other lines of work — industries adequate to the demands of Christian civilization, and nursery missions.

His plan in founding missions in Africa is to negotiate with kings and chiefs for mission-sites in suitable centres, with all the land needed for industrial school work,

and establish as a specialty a nursery mission on each site, placing in it a compe-
tent missionary matron, and adopting from
heathenism as quickly as possible from ten
to twenty little boys and girls before they
become heathens, and have them trained
from the beginning in the way in which
they should go.   The aim is, first, to train
them in suitable industries for self-support
in that country; second, to give them a
good common-school education; third, "to
get them quickly to the bosom of Jesus,
and thus enroll and equip them for the
good fight of faith;" and, fourth, to exercise them freely from the day of their
conversion "as witnesses for Jesus, and
soul-winners for his fold."

Self-support was achieved in India from
the start, on the Scripture principle that the
laborer is worthy of his hire; the church
being formed mainly from converts from
among the Eurasians, who were enabled
from their industries to contribute regu-
larly to the support of their missionaries,
and for the extension of the work among
the purely native population.

In South America the establishment of a high grade of schools formed an entering wedge, and furnished support for the missionaries.

In Africa it is different, the raw heathen having no means of supporting, or appreciation of, gospel preaching and school teaching. Bishop Taylor introduced such industries as were best adapted to the various parts of the continent where he opened missions, requiring, therefore, a longer or shorter period of time for their development. Coffee culture is the main industry on the west coast, requiring six or seven years to become profitably productive. The existing stations on this district have from one thousand to ten thousand coffee-trees each, the average subsidy required last year being a thousand dollars, exclusive of buildings.

On the Congo the farms are of necessity smaller; three of the missions there being self-supporting, and the others nearly so, except expenses for buildings and transportation. In the Province of Angola, mainly on the commercial plan, all the missions and stations, except the receiving stations at Loanda, are entirely self-supporting, and to a considerable extent self-propagating. Besides the profitable lines mentioned, the natives are everywhere taught all the varied industries of the house, shop, and farm, — the gain to them in developing a right spirit of independence and acquiring the practical knowledge of useful vocations exceeding the financial advantage to the mission.

The nursery missions are realizing the faith of their founder in the conversion of the children themselves, and their utilization as an evangelizing agency. By them, heathen, from kings and chiefs to outcast "bushmen," whose polygamous complications and adherence to various forms of witchcraft seemed a bar to the earnest efforts of the missionaries, have been led into the fold of Christ. These children, with the native evangelists, some of whom have been developed from the nursery missions, are everywhere one of the largest human agencies in the work of salvation. This was beautifully illustrated at a baptismal service at Brooks Mission, Liberia, where three generations of one family knelt at the head of the line of converts at the altar, — the grandmother, father and mother, and younger sister of Diana, the little Grebo girl who was introduced to the last General Conference.

All of Bishop Taylor's missionaries, together with the rapidly increasing number of native evangelists, receive no salary ; and yet a larger number than can be furnished with outfit, passage, mission-houses, and equipment, answer the constant call for more missionaries on the high line of voluntary surrender of legal rights for the establishment of the work.

Bishop Taylor declares that the evangelization of Africa is too big a contract for any one man or generation of men, but that his call is to introduce practical methods that will go on to the conquest of the midnight empire of the world for Christ after his " departure."

XIX.

ROBERT MOFFAT.

Missionary in Africa.

Born Dec. 21, 1795; Died Aug. 10, 1883.

XIX.

ROBERT MOFFAT.

" From scenes like these old Scotia's grandeur springs,
 That makes her loved at home, revered abroad ;
Princes and lords are but the breath of kings,
' An honest man's the noblest work of God ; '
  And certes, in fair Virtue's heavenly road,
  The cottage leaves the palace far behind."

LOOKING backward, Robert Moffat could clearly trace the trend of his life's purposes to the gentle but unconscious influence of his mother, who, in the little cottage home at Carronshore, Scotland, gathered her lads around the fireside on winter nights, while she read aloud accounts of missionary labors in heathen lands. Born Dec. 21, 1795, Robert had few educational advantages ; and, living in the midst of shipping, he early turned from "Wully Mitchell's" teaching of the

"Shorter Catechism," and "went to sea." In the peril of wind and waves many dangers were mentioned by him, and hairbreadth escapes chronicled; but to his parents' joy he gave up nautical pursuits, and entered school at Falkirk.

When but fourteen years old he was apprenticed to a gardener. His work was laborious, and his comforts scanty; yet withal he attended an evening school, and learned something of Latin and mensuration. Two years later he was employed as under gardener by Mr. Leigh, of High Leigh, Cheshire; and there, at the meetings of the Wesleyan Methodists, Robert became converted. Soon after his conversion some duty took him to Warrington, six miles distant; and as he crossed the bridge to the town, he saw a placard announcing a missionary meeting, to be held under the direction of the Rev. Wm. Roby of Manchester. Thoughts of his mother's reading, in the long ago, flooded his memory; and the determination to devote his life to missionary work was instantly

formed. Later, an interview with Mr.
Roby resulted in Moffat accepting a position in Mr. Smith's nursery garden, at
Durkinfield, near Manchester; and then he
began to prepare himself for the mission-
field under the care of Mr. Roby. While
thus at work, Robert became engaged to
his employer's daughter, Mary Smith.

A year later Robert Moffat went to
Manchester for a few months of college
training, and then accepted a position under the London Missionary Society, and
with four co-laborers sailed for South
Africa, Oct. 18, 1816. Cape Town was
reached Jan. 13, 1817; and while waiting
for a passport from the government to go
into the interior, Moffat boarded in a farm-
er's family at Stellenbosch, and passed his
time in acquiring the Dutch language,
which enabled him to preach to the Boers.

In September, in company with Mr. and
Mrs. Kichingman, Moffat, in charge of a
long trail of wagons drawn by oxen, started
for the Namaqualand Mission. The natives
at this station were ruled by Africaner, an

outlaw, and a terror to the farmers of the colony, but friendly to the English. After a dreary march, during which many of the oxen became prey to the hyenas, the band of missionaries reached Bysondermeid. Here Robert Moffat remained with the Kichingmans for a month, and then, aided by a guide, proceeded to the interior. The way inland lay through a trackless desert. Here the oxen became so exhausted, a halt was called before water could be reached, and Moffat was obliged to send to Mr. Bartlett at Pella for oxen accustomed to travel in deep sand. "Three days," says Robert Moffat, "I remained with my wagon-driver on this burning plain, with scarcely a breath of wind, and what there was felt as if coming from the mouth of an oven." Jan. 26, 1818, the train reached Afri-caner's kraal, and received a warm welcome from Mr. Ebner, who, a few days after, was obliged to depart, leaving Robert Moffat, a stranger in the midst of a strange people; but the heart of the young missionary was soon cheered by the regular attendance of Africaner at the religious services, and his conversion was followed by two of his brothers, who became such efficient assistants in the school and mission services that Moffat was soon able to undertake itinerating visits. These journeys were frequently attended by dangers and privations, and an indomitable will alone sustained life.

Two trips, to find a more healthful location for the mission, were unsuccessfully made ; and for twelve months Moffat lived and labored at Namaqualand as missionary, as carpenter, smith, cooper, shoemaker, miller, baker, and housekeeper.

In 1819 Moffat decided to visit Cape Town for supplies, and to introduce Africaner to the notice of the Colonial Government. To get the outlaw through the territories of the Dutch farmers, where his former atrocities were not forgotten, required nerveful tact, but was successfully done, and Africaner was cordially welcomed by the governor at Cape Town. Moffat had intended to return to Namaqualand, but yielded to the wish of the London

Missionary Society deputation then at Cape Town, to accompany them in their visits to missionary stations, and later to accept a mission at the Bechwana station. Africaner, hoping to move his tribe to Moffat's new station, journeyed home alone, conveying in his wagon, presented by the governor, many of the effects destined for the future field. The deputation, after visiting stations in the eastern part of the colony and at Kafirland, were barred from further progress by war, and returned to Cape Town. Here, on the 27th of December, 1819, Robert Moffat received his affianced wife, and soon after her arrival they were married.

At the beginning of the year 1820, the Moffats, with the Rev. John Campbell, started for the Bechwana station at Lattakoo, but were detained at Griqua Town for several months; and here was born their daughter Mary, afterwards the wife of Dr. Livingstone.

In May, 1821, Mr. and Mrs. Moffat arrived at Lattakoo, and commenced their work among a people who were "thoroughly sensual, and who could rob, lie, and murder without any compunctions of con-science, as long as success attended their efforts."

In 1822 Moffat wrote: "They turn a deaf ear to the voice of love, and scorn the doctrines of salvation, but affairs in general assume a more hopeful aspect. They have in several instances relinquished the bar-barous system of *commandoes* for stealing cattle. They have also dispensed with a rain-maker this season."

A little later in the same year, Robert Moffat said, "Mary, this is hard work, and no fruit yet appears;" and his wife wisely answered, "The gospel has not yet been preached to them in their own tongue in which they were born." From that time Moffat devoted himself to the acquisition of the language, and for that purpose he often visited tribes remote from his station.

No words can tell of the labors of Robert and Mary Moffat in these early days. In addition to privations, discour-

agements, and loss of property, their lives
were often in danger.   Once, when no rain
fell, these missionaries were accused of
causing the drought, and at the point of the
spear were told to leave the land.   Throwing open his waistcoat, Robert Moffat said
(fortified by the courage of his wife, who
stood at the door of their cottage with her
baby in her arms), " If you will, drive your
spear to my heart. We know you will
not touch our wives and children."   The
would-be murderers turned away, saying,
" These men must have ten lives, when
they are so fearless of death."   The good
will of the tribe was at last gained by the
able efforts of the missionaries in planning
a defence against the Mantatees, who attacked the station with murderous intent.
Deeply sensible of the kindness of the Moffats, who might at this time have retired to
the colony, the Bechwanas gave their consent to moving the station to a place eight
miles distant, at the source of the river
Kuruman.   In view of proper remu-
neration, the Bechwana chiefs arranged

that two miles of the Kuruman Valley should henceforth be the property of the London Missionary Society, and that the new station, " Kuruman," should here be established.

Referring to this time, Robert Moffat afterwards said : " Our situation during the infancy of the new station, language cannot describe. We were compelled to work daily at every species of labor." Notwithstanding all difficulties, this earnest man made considerable progress towards establishing a literature in the Sechwana tongue. A spelling-book and catechism were prepared, and sent to England to be printed. In 1826, having moved into his new dwelling, built of stone, and the country being comparatively free from danger, Moffat left his family, and went for a time to live among the Barolongs, that he might become proficient in the Sechwana language. While among these tribes, the missionary sought every opportunity to impart Christian instruction to the people.

Ten years the Moffats labored without seeing any results, when suddenly, without apparent cause, a great religious interest arose among the natives; the little chapel became too small to hold the numbers who came to receive the gospel. By voluntary aid, a new building, fifty-one feet by sixteen feet, with clay walls and thatched roof, was erected, and served as schoolhouse and place of worship until the large stone church was completed. A change of habits instantly followed this awakening. Mrs. Moffat was called upon to open a sewing-school, and motley were the groups gathered about her, all anxious to form garments to wear, although jackets, trousers, and gowns had never before adorned their forms.

When a friend at home wrote to Mary Moffat, asking what could be sent her that would be of use, the answer was, " Send a Communion service; it will be wanted." At that time there were no converts and no " glimmer of day." Three years later, a hundred and twenty were present at the table of the Lord, the first among the

Bechwanas; and the day previous there arrived a box which contained the Communion vessels which the faith of Mrs. Moffat had led her to ask for before there was a single inquirer.

In the fall of 1829 two envoys came from Mosilikatse, King of the Matabele, to learn about the manners and teachings of the white men. Later, Mr. Moffat visited this tribe, was kindly received, and told to them the story of the Resurrection. In June, 1830, Moffat had finished the translation of St. Luke; and to get this printed, and to place their two eldest children at school, Mr. and Mrs. Moffat went to Cape Town. Here Robert Moffat acquired a fair knowledge of printing, and applied himself so assiduously to the work, that a severe illness followed. This and the birth of another daughter delayed the missionaries; but in June, 1831, they returned to Kuruman, and took with them an edition of St. Luke, and a hymn-book in Sechwana, a printing-press, and liberal subscriptions for the erection of the mission-church. The

timber for this church was cut and collected under supervision of Mr. Hamilton
and Mr. Edwards, two hundred and fifty
·miles from the Kuruman Station, and
brought there in ox-teams. This church
was opened November, 1838, and nine
hundred people were in attendance at the
first service ; the following Sunday a hundred and fifty members celebrated the
Lord's Supper.

In the spring of 1839 Robert Moffat
completed the translation of the New
Testament, and for purposes of printing
went to England with his wife, after an
absence of twenty-two years. During the
voyage another daughter was born to
them, and their son Jamie, six years old,
died. The Moffats received a very warm
welcome in England ; and at this time
"a wave of missionary enthusiasm" swept
over the country, and great was the
demand for Mr. Moffat to address public meetings. While in England, it was
thought best to add the Psalms to the
Sechwana edition of the New Testament ;

and with characteristic energy, Moffat immediately began the work of translating, and sent to Ross and David Livingstone, then at Bechwana Mission, six thousand copies of the new work. Moffat then wrote his well-known book, " Missionary Labors and Scenes in South Africa ; " and it was not until January, 1843, that he and Mrs. Moffat sailed for Africa. The natives at Kuruman received them with unbounded joy.

Soon after their return their eldest daughter, Mary, was married to David Livingstone, and went with him to Chonwane. Affairs at the Kuruman were now very prosperous. Moffat worked steadily at translation ; Mrs. Moffat, his faithful helpmate, leaving him only to visit the Livingstones and to go to Cape Town with her youngest children, who were going to England to be educated. In 1856 Moffat completed his translation of the entire Bible, a work of thirty years.

" I felt it to be an awful thing," he says, " to translate the Book of God. When I had finished the last verse, I could hardly believe that I was in the world, so difficult was it for me to realize that my work of so many years was completed. A feeling came over me as if I should die. . . . My heart beat like the strokes of a hammer. . . . My emotions found vent by my falling on my knees, and thanking God for his grace and goodness for giving me strength to accomplish my task."

At this time Livingstone was in England ; and, as a result of his accounts, the directors wrote to Robert Moffat asking him to go for twelve months to Matabele. In spite of the fact that he had worked for the company forty-one years, and was then sixty-two years old, Robert Moffat left his home at Kuruman, and started for a long and toilsome journey through the African desert. He spent many months at " Inyati," the seat of the missions of the Matabele, and spared neither labor of body nor mind. In June, 1860, feeling the station was well established, he returned to Kuruman. In 1862 Robert and Mary Moffat suffered severe bereavement in the death of their son Robert, and of their daughter Mary Livingstone. In 1868, having established his son, the Rev. John Moffat, at Kuruman, Robert Moffat determined, reluctantly, to accept the directors' invitation to return to England. On Sunday, March 20, 1870, he preached for the last time in the Kuruman church; and the following Friday "Ramary" and "Mamary," as the dearly beloved missionary and his wife were called, left the home in which they had so long and so faithfully labored, amid a pitiful wail from the natives, whose hearts were wrung with genuine sorrow.

July 24, 1870, Robert and Mary Moffat arrived in England, after an absence of over fifty years, during which time they had visited their native land but once. They were welcomed everywhere with marked cordiality, and on his birthday a thousand pounds was given Mr. Moffat. A few months after their return Mary Moffat died. Her last words were a prayer for her husband, that he might be given strength to bear her loss. Fifty-three years she had faithfully shared his labors. In 1872 several thousand pounds were subscribed for a training-school for natives in Bechwana; and the directors honored their veteran missionary by calling it the "Moffat Institute." Later his friends gave to Robert Moffat five thousand pounds, a liberal competency for himself and his widowed daughter, Mrs. Frédoux. In 1874 Mr. Moffat was called upon to identify the remains of his son-in-law, Dr. Livingstone, who had died in Central Africa. In 1876 Mr. Moffat was entertained by the Archbishop of Canterbury, and by the Rev. Newman Hall, where he met Mr. Gladstone. In 1877 he visited Paris, and addressed four thousand Sunday-school children.

The last four years of his life were spent at Park Cottage, Leigh, near Tunbridge.

On the 10th of August, 1883, in his eighty-eighth year, he passed peacefully to rest.

> " His count of years was full ;
> His allotted task was wrought."

As a fitting close to this sketch I quote

from the pen of the Rev. A. C. Thompson,
D.D., of Boston, who was present at the
World's Missionary Conference in London
in 1878 : —

"'Nothing but a missionary!' But the man
who gave that toss of the head and that half scorn-
ful look should cast an eye down the long centre
aisle of the hall at Mildmay Park. Whom do we
see coming up the aisle — a son of Anak in stature,
erect, his features strongly marked, his venerable
locks and long white beard adding majesty to his
appearance? On discovering him the whole great
audience rise spontaneously to their feet. A Wesleyan brother with powerful voice is in the midst of
an address; yet no one heeds him till the patriarch
has taken a seat on the platform. Who is the old
man? Is it the Earl of Beaconsfield? Is it Mr.
Gladstone? There is but one other person in the
realm, I take it, to whom, under the circumstances,
such a united and enthusiastic tribute would be
paid, and that because she is on the throne. This
hoary-headed man is the veteran among South
African missionaries. He went out to the Dark
Continent more than sixty years before (1816). He
is now eighty-three; his name Robert Moffat. . . .
With a voice still strong and musical he addresses
the assembly for twenty or more minutes. The man
who preaches to a larger congregation than any other
in London once said that, when he saw the veteran
Moffat, he felt inclined to sink into his shoes."

XX.

WILLIAM McCLURE THOMSON.

Missionary in Syria.

Born Dec. 31, 1806; Died April 8, 1894.

XX.

WILLIAM McCLURE THOMSON.

"THE Land and the Book!" Who that
loves the Book of books has not longed to
wander, at least in fancy, over the land of
its birth, and through familiarity with its
scenes, its customs, its history, gain clearer
understanding of its meaning? And who
that has mentally traversed that sacred
country under the guidance of the veteran
missionary, William M. Thomson, has not
wished for closer acquaintance with a man
whose life was bound up in the country of
his adoption?

To know him well, intimately, was to ad-
mire and love him. He came of sturdy
Scotch-Irish stock, inheriting therefrom
an indomitable persistency that carried
him over many obstacles, and, added to
his natural capacity for research, made

him indefatigable in his archæological studies.

His father was the Rev. John Thomson, who went from Ohio to Kentucky in the early part of this century; but so strong were the anti-slavery principles of both himself and his wife that they found it impossible to live in a slave State, and returned to Ohio. There, in the little village of Springfield (now Spring Dale), near Cincinnati, William McClure Thomson was born, on Dec. 31, 1806. At the age of twenty he graduated from the Miami University, and then entered Princeton Theological Seminary, where he was one of the pupils of Dr. Archibald Alexander.

He did not graduate from the Seminary. He had given himself to mission-work, and the call was pressing. His license to preach was granted him; and, under the direction of the American Board, he sailed for Syria, reaching Beirut Feb. 24, 1833. With him was his wife, formerly Miss Eliza Nelson Hanna, whose tragic death at Jerusalem was so soon to follow.

The young missionaries were stationed at once at that place, and entered upon their work with zeal ; but Syria was in a disturbed condition, and the following year the troubles between the people of Syria and Ibrahim Pasha (son of the famous Mohammed Ali) culminated in open warfare. Dr. Thomson had started on a tour to Jaffa, expecting to be absent only a short time, but was arrested as a spy by Ibrahim, and detained forty days. Meantime the fighting in and about Jerusalem was very severe. The few foreign residents, among whom was Mrs. Thomson, were lodged in a small building directly beneath the walls of the castle, which was the main point of attack and defence. The cannonading was carried on directly over their heads, day and night, balls now and then crashing into the upper part of the dwelling, obliging them all to remain in a sort of vault beneath the house, not knowing at what moment the walls might come tumbling about them. To the terrors of the siege were added those of a severe earthquake, and Mrs. Thomson received a nervous shock from which she never recovered. A journal letter written to her sister in America during the siege presents a vivid picture of the horrors of those weeks, but is as calm and even in its unfaltering trust as if written in the most tranquil ease.

After the fall of Jerusalem, Dr. Thomson was released, but found his wife critically ill, and she lived but a short time.

With his infant son he then returned to Beirut, where he subsequently married Mrs. Abbott, the widow of a former British consul for Syria. Here, in 1837, the first boarding-school for boys in the Turkish Empire was opened under the direction of Dr. Thomson and Mr. Hebard.

A little later he was appointed one of two to form a mission station in Lebanon, and resided in Abeih, where he passed through the wars between Druses and Maronites in 1843 and 1845. He was looked upon as a friend by both parties, and by his influence brought about a truce which enabled the British Consul-General, the late Sir Hugh Rose (Lord Strathnairn), to bring away the Maronites to Beirut, thus preventing a general massacre of Maronite Christians.

About the year 1850 he removed to Sidon, where he was stationed for several years, extending his missionary labors to Hermon, Ijon, and vicinity, and to the region east of Tyre. While at this point he received, in 1858, the degree of D.D. from Wabash College. In 1860, having returned to Beirut, he co-operated with Lord Dufferin, the representative of the allied forces, in adjusting matters after the massacres of Damascus, Hasbeiyeh, and Deir el Quamar.

But the culmination of his labors was " The Land and the Book," that magnificent work of which the *Bibliotheca Sacra* said : " If the Syrian mission had produced no other fruit, the churches which have supported it would have received in this book an ample return for all they have expended. The plan of the book is unique. It is a book of travels, a book of conversations, a running comment on the Scriptures, and a pictorial geography and history of Palestine, all in one."

It was first published, in two volumes, in 1859. In 1876, having again gone thoroughly over the ground and collected much new material, Dr. Thomson went to Edinburgh to supervise the issuing of the enlarged edition, described by Dr. Thomas Laurie as " not a wooden building repainted and patched up here and there, but a stone structure taken down to the foundation and rebuilt with much new material on a better plan." The new edition, in three volumes, was published simultaneously in New York and Edinburgh ; and its sales in Great Britain have been greater than those of any other American publication except " Uncle Tom's Cabin."

Dr. Thomson never returned to Syria. From Edinburgh he came to New York ; but before the third volume of his work was issued from the press his health began to show the effects of advancing years, and it was plain that his active physical labors were ended.

But "The Land and the Book" by no means represents the sum total of his literary labors. His contributions to the *Bibliotheca Sacra* were numerous and valuable, covering a wide range of subjects. Prominent among them was a series of articles on "The Natural Basis of our Spiritual Language." He also furnished to the *Journal of the American Oriental Society* an extremely interesting paper on traces of glacial action on Mount Lebanon. In the variety and value of his contributions to the geography of Syria, he was almost without a peer; and his co-laborer, Dr. C. V. A. Van Dyck, writes: "From the beginning of his missionary life he vigorously pursued archæological studies connected with the elucidation of Scripture, and became an authority on these points."

The phrase "vigorously pursued" is eminently characteristic of the way in which he attacked whatever lay before him. There was about him, especially in his youth, a vigor and even tempestuousness hard to realize by those who knew him

only in his later years, when he became
the embodiment of gentleness and placid-
ity.   A laughable story illustrating his
natural vehemence is told of him by a gentleman who accompanied him on one of
his tours.   They had camped for the night
on an extended plain ; and the start next
morning was, as always among the Arabs,
a scene of confusion.   Everything was
finally packed up, and Mr. —— rode on,
expecting the rest of the party to follow
almost immediately.   But after some time,
becoming puzzled by their non-appearance,
he rode back to ascertain the cause.   An
unregenerate mule — the one laden with
the kitchen furniture — had, at the last
moment, been possessed of an evil spirit,
and by a series of such kicks and antics as
only a Syrian mule is capable of, had scattered pots, pans, and all the rest of the
impedimenta in every direction, covering
an extent of country appalling to contemplate.   The muleteers were racing after it,
showering maledictions upon it and its
ancestors back to the time of the progeni-

tor who entered the Ark, while Dr. Thomson, in an excess of righteous indignation, was exclaiming, "I wish I had a cannon to shoot that mule!" As nothing short of a cannon would have been of the slightest service in relieving his feelings, and that ponderous weapon was not at hand, the lucky beast escaped all punishment save such thumps as were bestowed by its breathless driver, when at last he succeeded in grasping the halter.

In the early part of Dr. Thomson's missionary life he kept careful journals of his many tours; and these, which were published in the *Missionary Herald*, contain much of absorbing interest, and afford glimpses of the different phases of his many-sided character. In one of these journals is the following description of a sunrise over Lebanon: —

"While spending the hot months of summer at Brumana, Mr. Hebard and myself devoted a day to rambling over this goodly mountain; and to me it was a delightful excursion. We were early abroad, just as Lucifer, bright harbinger of morning, rising from his dreary couch, sat like a blazing diamond on the hoary head of Lebanon. We quickly despatched our little work of preparation, sipped our hot coffee, and sallied forth for the day's adventures. How surpassingly beautiful is the rosy dawn in Syria! From the moment when the advanced rays of the sun begin to paint the modest blush upon the dusky cheek of night, until the king of day comes forth from his chamber in the full majesty of his rising, there is one incessant change from beauty to beauty, yea, from glory to glory. The whole horizon glows like burnished gold, revealing the rocks and crags and lofty peaks of Lebanon throughout its whole extent. Every point seems touched with liquid fire, gleaming in seven-fold fervency, while the whole western slope, to the very base, falling into the dark shadow of her lofty summit, lay in deepest contrast to the living light above and beyond. Who can behold, and not adore? It is God's own temple, and yonder comes his bright messenger to call a sleeping world to prayer. Oh, come, let us worship and bow down, let us kneel before the Lord our maker. Let us come before his presence with thanksgiving, and show ourselves glad in him with psalms. For he is the Lord our God, and we are the people of his pasture and the sheep of his hand."

It is said that a missionary in the Hawaiian Islands, reading the above description, was so struck with its poetic beauty that, by a slight paraphrase, he divided it into lines of faultless blank verse, with scarcely the alteration of a word, and returned it to be republished in that form. The succeeding passage of the diary, though less rhythmical, is scarcely less striking in its imagery: —

"Our morning's ride furnished us with another and very different exhibition of God's handiwork. The cool wind, loaded with the condensed vapors of higher Lebanon, rushed down the mountain side, dashing and bursting, bounding and retreating from perpendicular cliffs, filling up deep valleys, and then pouring over the surrounding ridges like any other fluid. Thus these dark volumes rolled headlong towards the plain, until, meeting the warm air of the sea, they appeared to hesitate, then stop altogether, and, vanishing into thin air, ascend to the cooler regions above, where, reappearing, they were seen hurrying back towards the snowy summits of Suñ- ñeen. This process of decomposing and recompos- ing clouds, and their marching and counter-marching to the command of contrary currents of air, is wit- nessed very frequently in Lebanon."

A more fitting close to this sketch can- not be found than in the eloquent tribute

given by the Rev. Henry H. Jessup, D.D.,
of the Syrian Mission, in his address at
the annual meeting of the American Board,
at Madison, Wis., Oct. 11, 1894: —

"Two of your missionaries were the pioneers, in
modern times, in Palestine exploration. I need
hardly mention the names of Drs. William M.
Thomson and Eli Smith, the latter as the companion and co-laborer of Dr. Edward Robinson,
in the exploration of Palestine and the authorship
of that classic, the 'Biblical Researches,' and the
former the author of that monumental work, 'The
Land and the Book.'

"There was a divine providence in raising up
two such scholarly and accurate observers as Smith
and Thomson, to traverse repeatedly the whole
land of Syria and Palestine, to mark its mountains and valleys, its hills and ravines, its plains
and rivers, its fountains, wells, and lakes, its ruined
temples, walls, fortresses, bridges, and aqueducts;
to gather its minerals, plants, and animals; to study
the agricultural, mechanical, and domestic implements and customs of the people, their language
and salutations, their dress and ornaments, their
buying and selling, and their modes of travel, all of
which were, at that time, still existing in their patri-
archal and scriptural simplicity; yes, to observe all
these things accurately; to record them with scrupulous and scholarly exactness; and to publish them

with conscientious fidelity, so that their honest testimony as to the correspondence between the historical records of the Bible and the actual places, names, persons, and customs of modern Palestine might be incorporated in permanent form in American and European Bible dictionaries, encyclopædias, and commentaries before the advancing wave of Western civilization — with its wagon-roads, railways, telegraphs, steam-pumps, Européan languages and dress — should have obliterated forever the living testimony of the present to the dead and vanished past.

" Dr. Thomson returned to the United States in 1877, to complete his great work, and in 1890 took up his residence with his daughter in Denver, Colo., whose clear skies and towering mountains, he said, reminded him of his beloved Mount Lebanon. In that city he remained until April 8, 1894, when, at the good old age of eighty-seven, he was summoned to the heavenly Canaan, the unfading and unclouded 'Land of Promise,' by the Inspirer of the 'Book' he had so faithfully labored to illustrate and exalt before the minds of his fellow-men."

XXI.

MARCUS WHITMAN, M. D.

Missionary in Oregon.

BORN SEPT. 4, 1802; DIED NOV. 29, 1847.

DR. MARCUS WHITMAN AT THE TIME OF HIS MARRIAGE.

XXI.

MARCUS WHITMAN, M.D.

IF the magnitude of a man's work is to be judged by its far-reaching results, surely that accomplished by Marcus Whitman, missionary to Oregon, must take rank among the great achievements of the world's benefactors ; and the heart of every true American must throb with gratitude and pride when he contemplates the effects of this " brave man's deed and word." Inspired by the highest motive, that of carrying the gospel to those in darkness, he entered upon his work with all the enthusiasm of his hardy and generous nature.

In the year 1832 an Indian chief, who had come to St. Louis in search of the white man's " Book of God," before returning to his people, in a farewell address said : " I came to you over a trail of many moons from the setting sun. My people sent me to get the white man's Book of Heaven. You showed me images of good spirits, and pictures of the good land beyond, but the Book was not among them to tell me the way. . . . My people will die in darkness, and they will go on the trail to the other hunting-grounds. No white man will go with them, and no white man's book to make the way plain. I have no more words."

This speech was delivered to a few hearers in a store-room belonging to the American Fur Company, where they were gathering preparatory to starting on their annual expedition to the far West, with whom the lonely Indian was to make his return journey. One of the listeners in this little audience was a young clerk in the office, whose heart was moved by the sad refrain ; and, when writing to his friend in Pittsburg, he described the pathetic scene and reported the speech. After a time, when the accuracy of the incident

had been proven, this speech was given to
the public, with the hope that it might
arouse an interest in missionary enterprise
among the Indians.

Originating from this pathetic cry, the
call came to the Rev. Samuel Parker, a cul-
tivated gentleman and devoted minister in
Ithaca, N.Y., who was the first to offer
himself to the American Board as a missionary to Oregon, in 1834. He went East
to induce others to join him, and there
found Dr. Whitman, to whom the appeal
came as a divine call; and as a live coal
from God's altar it kindled in his heart a
mighty zeal, which carried him through all
future hardships and dangers.

He was born at Rushville, N.Y., Sept.
4, 1802, and was "reared amid the environments of a pioneer home, and made
familiar with the privations incident to such
a life." He received the best possible religious training from his parents at home;
and after the death of his father, which
occurred when Marcus was only eight years
of age, it was continued with scrupulous

care by his grandfather, Deacon Samuel Whitman, of Plainville, Mass.

He began study, having the ministry in view, but, on account of physical ailments, turned to the study of medicine, and in due time received his degree of M.D.

Dr. Whitman was past thirty years of age when his thoughts were turned toward Oregon. He had spent four years in the practice of medicine, and some years in business, having been part owner with his brother of a sawmill, an experience most valuable in later years in his missionary work.

Mr. Parker and Dr. Whitman started for Oregon in the summer of 1835, travelling with the party sent out by the American Fur Company, as far as Green River in Wyoming. This was the terminus of the Fur Company's route, and a meeting-place for traders, trappers, and a multitude of Indians from all parts of the great wilderness. Here they came annually to exchange their year's collection of furs for the necessities and luxuries of life, brought overland by the company from the States. During their stay of several days here, through intercourse with these various representatives of the wild country to which they were bound, and with the knowledge they had gained on their long journey, the missionaries were able to more fully comprehend the nature and magnitude of the work which they were about to undertake. They now realized that a stronger force and better equipment were necessary. It was therefore decided that Dr. Whitman should return to the East with the company's party, and secure re-enforcements; while Mr. Parker should proceed to Oregon, and select suitable locations for the three missions which they proposed to establish. Dr. Whitman took with him three Nez Perces boys, and, returning to central New York, made an earnest effort to enlist the interest of his friends.

He now saw, as he was entering upon his life-work, that an important factor in this new mission must be the Christian home ; and before going West again he was married to Miss Narcissa Prentice, daughter of Judge Stephen Prentice of Prattsburg, N.Y., who is described as "a handsome, refined, and accomplished young lady, a beautiful singer, and possessing the spirit of a true heroine." The marriage occurred in March, and the next month they started on their long wedding-tour.

With them also went the Rev. H. H. Spaulding and his young bride, and Mr. Wm. H. Gray, the latter going as mechanic and business agent for the mission. These two heroic women — the first to cross the Rocky Mountains — little realized at that time the full significance of their journey to Oregon. To them it meant reaching the heathen with a message; to us it meant a vastly enlarged territory and an entire change in the character of its population.

An immense section of the Pacific coast, consisting of about three hundred thousand square miles, had for years been in possession of the Hudson Bay Company, who, with their forts and trading-posts, had driven out eleven fur companies who had sought to establish trade in that country. It was a powerful monopoly, whose policy was to keep the country in its present wild state for the sake of the fur products. Consequently, all immigration of families from the East was discouraged.

When these missionary families crossed the mountains, and opened the way for others to follow, it was the beginning of a new era — the establishment of a civilization which was entirely to displace the unnatural and peculiar social order then existing.

Much had been said to discourage their undertaking. It is said that advice to turn back, warnings as well as prayers and benedictions, followed them from place to place before leaving the States.

They joined a group of the American Fur Company at Council Bluffs, and continued with them to the end of the route at Green River. These men at first were not pleased at the idea of admitting ladies into their caravan. They did not think it

possible for them to endure the wearisome
and perilous journey; but, on account of
the valuable medical services rendered by
Dr. Whitman on his previous trip, they
gave consent.   All through the long journey, these noble and high-minded women
were treated with the greatest deference
by the men of the company, who tried in
every possible way to lessen the hardships
of the trip.   Mrs. Spaulding suffered much
from fatigue, and it was feared at one time
that she would not live, as she was taken
fainting from her saddle; but her courage
was phenomenal, and carried her through.
One of the rough men said, in speaking of
these brave women, "There is something
which the Honorable Hudson Bay Company cannot expel from the country."

On the Fourth of July they reached the
famous South Pass, Nature's gateway
through the mighty wall, which she has
kindly left, that the country may not be
divided.

This is an interesting spot, where two
rivers, one flowing toward the Pacific, the

other toward the Atlantic, have their source within half a mile of each other. Here upon a rock are carved the names of noted travellers, such as " Fremont, 1843," and " Stanbury, 1849." Barrows, in his history of Oregon, says, " It may give information and divide honors with the ' Pathfinder ' to add ' Mesdames Whitman and Spaulding, 1836.' " Six years before a company of United States engineers had seen this pass, two women had gone through.

When they had crossed the Continental Divide, and were on the Pacific side of the slope, the missionary party dismounted, planted the American flag, and, kneeling on their blankets about the " Book," with prayer and praise they took possession of the western slope for Christ and the Church. This was, indeed, a most significant action when viewed in the light of subsequent history. The Rev. Jonathan Edwards, in speaking of this scene, says, " How strongly it evidences their faith in their mission, and the conquering power of the King of peace. A scene truly inspiring to contemplate, and worthy a place on the canvas among the masterpieces of the world's great artists." It was an act, the far-reaching consequences of which secured to the United States three hundred thousand square miles of the Pacific Coast.

A few days more of travel brought them to Green River and to the annual gathering, the fair and festival of the mountains. To the ladies this was a novel experience. The Indian wigwams stretching for three miles along the river, the encampment of trappers and traders, with about twenty citizens, including the missionary families, making in all fifteen hundred persons. To many of these rough trappers, whose home for twenty-five years had been in the depths of these forests and in the cañons of the mountains, it was also a novel experience to meet a lady; and many of them were moved to tears, being reminded of loved ones far away in the old home. One of these men, years after, said, " From that day, when I took the hand of à civilized woman again, I was a better man."

Here the party rested for ten days. They wrote letters home, to be sent back with the returning company of traders, repacked and reduced their baggage, and prepared for their further journey.

Dr. Whitman was warmly welcomed by the Indians whom he had met there the year before, and who were expecting him according to promise. From this point the party were escorted by traders from the Hudson Bay Company on their way back to the Pacific coast from the annual meeting.

They next stopped at Fort Hall, and again reduced and repacked baggage. In a few days they reached Fort Boisé, where, by the advice of the Hudson Bay Company, the doctor left his wagon. This wagon was the first to be taken farther than Fort Laramie, and it was destined to play a very important part in the history of Oregon and the Pacific Coast. " Whitman's wagon had demonstrated that women and children and household goods — the family — could be carried over the plains and mountains to Oregon." If so, the United States wanted Oregon.

The mission party reached Fort Walla Walla early in September; and the long journey of thirty-five hundred miles, begun four months before, was ended. Dr. Whitman established a mission among the Cayuse tribe on the Walla Walla River, six miles west of the present city of Walla Walla, giving to the settlement the name of Waiilatpu. Mr. Spaulding settled at Clear Water, and established another mission among the Nez Perces tribe, a few miles north of the Kooskooskie River. These were two of the sites which had been chosen by the Rev. Mr. Parker, who, after spending a year in Oregon, preparing the way for the missionaries, returned to his home by way of the Hawaiian Islands. It had been the intention of the missionaries to establish one of the missions among the Flatheads; but, on account of the unsettled condition of the tribe at that time, it was not deemed wise to venture among them. The Whitmans were gladly welcomed by the Cayuse Indians, and in a short time the mission was well established and in a prosperous condition.

In three years' time they had two hundred and fifty acres of land enclosed, of which two hundred acres were in a good state of cultivation. A grist-mill had been constructed, an orchard planted, and their third building was in progress of erection. Fifty or more of the Indian children had been gathered into a school, which Mrs. Whitman taught. For six years they labored, Mrs. Whitman giving her attention to the school and general work of the mission and home ; the doctor superintending the work of the farm and the mill, preaching and teaching, in addition to a large medical practice extending over many square miles.

Their work was difficult and trying, as these Indians were wild and superstitious, and more averse to settled life than were many of the tribes ; yet a large number of them had been induced to engage in agriculture.

In the fall of 1842 the two missions, which had been re-enforced by two other missionaries, held their annual business meeting at this station. While it was in progress Dr. Whitman was called to attend a patient at Fort Walla Walla, twenty-five miles distant. This was an important trading-post, the fort belonging to the Hudson Bay Company. Here hospitality was dispensed most generously to all travellers; and it chanced at this time that there was an unusually large and congenial company present. Twenty or more of their men had arrived that day in charge of boats laden with Indian goods. These, with their traders and clerks, made a large company, in which Dr. Whitman was the only representative of the United States.

While they were seated at dinner a messenger arrived and announced to the company that a colony of British settlers from the Red River had crossed the mountains, and were then about three hundred miles up the Columbia River. This announcement was hailed with many expressions of delight, and congratulations passed from one to another; when, in the excitement, a young priest arose, and, waving his cap in

the air, cried " Hurrah for Oregon ; America is too late, and we have got the country ! " To Dr. Whitman this was not an
entirely new revelation of the state of
affairs. He had been impressed, six years
before, by the opposition of the company's
agents to his taking his wagon and farm-
ing implements through from Fort Boisé ;
and the same opposition had been met by
a company of immigrants the year before.
The president of the company had advised
that the Board would better send travelling
missionaries to the Indians and trappers,
rather than establish settled missions.

This unguarded statement from the
young priest confirmed him in the belief
that this company, since it could not prevent immigration, and thus preserve the
forests for hunting-grounds, had changed
its policy, and was now seeking to bring in
British subjects to take possession of the
country and keep Americans out. He was
now thoroughly aroused to the situation.
Something must be done, and at once.
This information must be carried to Wash-

ington, and colonies from the States must be brought in to occupy the lands, and save the country.

Hastening to his home, he called the missionaries together, and explaining his discovery to them, he announced his intention of going at once to Washington. They did not at first favor this plan; but, as he was determined, their confidence in the man led them to unanimous approval. A few years later they were able to see the emergency as he saw it then. Said Dr. Eells, " It was suggested to him that this was hardly within the legitimate work of the mission; to which he replied, that for this emergency he did not belong so much to the American Board as to his country." Within twenty-four hours from the scene at the dinner-table, Dr. Whitman was in his saddle headed for Washington, having arranged for the care of his wife and the mission during his absence.

This memorable ride must take rank with other pivotal events in our history; for, although it requires deeper thinking to realize its full import, it is, nevertheless, unequalled by any similar exhibition of patriotism, " distance, time, heroic daring, peril, suffering, and magnificent consequences."

Mr. Amos Lovejoy, who had recently arrived with a band of immigrants and a guide, accompanied Whitman with two pack mules to carry supplies. In eleven days they reached Fort Hall, having travelled three hundred and forty miles. They then travelled due south to reach the old Santa Fé trail, thinking to avoid the intense cold by going that way. Their course, in the main, was in the direction followed by the present Utah Southern railroad.

From Mr. Lovejoy's journal we have the following items : —

" From Fort Hall to Fort Vinta we had terribly severe weather. Passing over the high mountains we encountered a terrible snow-storm, compelling us to seek refuge for ten days in a dark defile. While in this defile, Dr. Whitman became impatient to move on, and against the guide's counsel they started. For some time they wandered in the snow, and the guide acknowledged that he was lost.   In the blinding snow-storm, not knowing where to turn, Whitman gave up for the first and only time, but suddenly the guide noticed a peculiar movement of one of the mule's ears. He said that mule knew how to find the way back to the defile they had left. Giving the reins to the animal, they were led back to the refuge, where they found the embers of their fire."

As soon as possible Whitman went back to Fort Taos, where he procured another guide; then they pushed on again.   At one time they came to a river two hundred yards wide, which was frozen over about one-third the distance on either side. Without hesitating an instant, Whitman and his horse plunged in and were soon on the other side.

Dr. Whitman reached St. Louis in due time, dressed in his buckskin breeches and fur garments; and, like a hero fresh from the battle-field, he bore many marks of the severity of the weather, and the hardships and perils through which he had passed.   From St. Louis he went by stage to Washington, arriving there March 3, 1843.

Haste was imperative, and what urged him to press on through driving storms, amid perils and hardships, was the impending boundary treaty between Canada and the United States. There was danger of Oregon being given away. Dr. Whitman felt that he must show Congress the value of Oregon, and demonstrate to that body and to those in authority the possibilities of colonizing the region. He thought he must reach Washington before this treaty, which affected the boundary, was concluded. This he failed to do in spite of his heroic work; yet his journey was not in vain, for the treaty had not touched upon the Oregon boundary.

He therefore had time to correct many erroneous ideas in regard to Oregon, and to expose the scheme of the Hudson Bay Company to capture the region by colonization. To show that information was needed in Washington, we quote a few sentences from the debate in Congress. Said one, " I would not give a pinch of snuff for the whole of Oregon for agricultural purposes, and I thank God that he put the Rocky Mountains between it and the east." Another said, "All the gold mines of Peru would not pay a penny on a pound of the cost it would be to build a railroad across the mountains to Oregon."

In Washington, Dr. Whitman called on Daniel Webster, who at that time was Secretary of State, and told his thrilling story. The great statesman replied, "Wagons cannot cross the mountains. Sir G. Simpson, who is here, affirms that, and so do all his correspondents in that region. Besides, I am about trading that worthless territory for some valuable concessions in relation to the Newfoundland cod-fisheries." Dr. Whitman replied, "Mr. Webster, we want that valuable territory ourselves." He then went to President Tyler, and said the same thing. The President replied, "Since you are a missionary, I will believe you; and if you take your emigrants over there, the treaty will not be ratified."

A secondary object of this journey was

to lead back to Oregon a colony. By
doing so he could settle by actual proof
the accessibility of that far Western district. On his way to Washington he
published pamphlets and newspaper articles telling of this proposed party. In
every town he passed through he urged
the people to organize and go West, and
meet him at Westport, Mo., when he
returned in the spring. Some of his cir-
culars went as far south as Texas.

Another object of the trip was to consult with the American Board in regard to
the missions, and to get re-enforcements
and money. The Prudential Committee
had voted to give up the mission station;
but, after hearing Dr. Whitman's report,
"it was resolved to sustain the operations of the mission without any material
change."

When he reached Westport, which was
the starting-point of Western immigration,
he found a company of eight hundred and
seventy-one persons with a hundred and
eleven wagons and two thousand head of

cattle and horses, ready to start on the long journey, in response to his appeal made on the way East. " On that journey," says Mr. Spaulding, " Dr. Whitman was their everywhere-present angel of mercy, ministering to the sick, helping the weary, encouraging the wavering, cheering the mothers, mending wagons, setting broken bones, finding stray oxen ; now in the rear, now in the centre, now in front, looking out fords ; in the dark mountains working out passages at noontide or at midnight, as though these were his own children and these wagons and flocks his own property." The entire company reached Oregon in safety.

As is often the case with our greatest benefactors, and those that live in advance of their times, it was not given Dr. Whitman to enjoy the fruits of his own magnificent achievements. That which gave him the greatest joy and satisfaction because of its promise of greatest ultimate good to the people for whom he was giving his life without stint, was one of the causes of

his own destruction. The colony which
he had been instrumental in raising and
bringing through, that great advance-
guard of civilization which was to follow,
and thus secure and save Oregon, was not
pleasing to the Indian. He saw in it the
melting away of his own tribe. The Indian had always been averse to civilization. He did not object to the trappers,
for they entered into Indian life and customs, and troubled them not by visions of
a better life. The traders were also welcomed; for they furnished a little variety
to their lives, and brought rude comforts
to them, and gave them a market for their
own wares. The Hudson Bay Company
had been welcomed to their country; for
its policy had always been to court the
good-will of the savages, and they had
opposed the settlement of the country,
and, with the Indians, wished to preserve
it as a wilderness. Nor did the Roman
Catholic priest meet the same opposition
as did the Protestant missionary with his
family. The priest came without family,

and therefore did not seem to be so much in opposition to the Indian's wild life.

But Dr. Whitman had brought the colony, and the colonists had brought the measles among them. This disease had spread among the Indians, very many of whom died from it because of their ignorance in caring for the sick. We are told that in the height of the fever the afflicted ones would frequently plunge into the stream for relief, after which, of course, the doctor's medicine could not cure. Then said they, " The doctor cures the white man, but not the Indian ; therefore the doctor gives the Indian poison." That seemed to them good reasoning, and it was talked of and brooded over until the dark plot was evolved to take the lives of the entire missionary family (it is the old story) ; and so the one who was really doing the most for them, working day and night to give them medical aid and teach them the way of life, was looked upon by them as their worst enemy.

Nov. 29, 1847, occurred the massacre of

Dr. Whitman, his noble wife, and twelve others, all of whom belonged to the mission. This was one of the saddest events in the history of Oregon or the Pacific Coast. The doctor had attended the funeral of an Indian in the morning, and, returning to the mission-house, was caring for his three adopted children, who were very ill. Early in the afternoon, a savage came in the house and called for Dr. Whitman. Soon after, the chief, Ti-lau-kait, came in and engaged the doctor in conversation, while another Indian stole in, and, with his tomahawk, struck the missionary a blow on the head. We shall not dwell upon this scene of blood and death. Mrs. Whitman was shot by a young Indian who had received special kindness at her hand. Having tasted blood, and their savage natures having full play, with clubs, knives, and tomahawks, they continued their work of death and torture eight days, until fourteen lives were sacrificed.

Thus ends the life-work of Marcus and

Narcissa Whitman, two of the most consecrated, successful, and heroic missionaries
ever sent out by any missionary society.
Dr. Whitman was only forty-five years of
age when he suffered the death of a martyr, but he had accomplished enough for
the life-work of one man.   He had saved
Oregon to the United States, and given
the gospel to the Indians and the white
pioneers of the Pacific Coast.   As a fitting
monument to the memory of this heroic
missionary, intrepid pathfinder, and far-
seeing patriot, a Christian college has
been established at Walla Walla, Wash.,
which bears the revered name of Marcus
Whitman.

XXII.

BISHOP JAMES HANNINGTON.

Missionary to Africa.

Born Sept. 3, 1847; Died Oct. 28, 1885.

XXII.

BISHOP JAMES HANNINGTON.

BISHOP JAMES HANNINGTON was born Sept. 3, 1847, at St. George, Hurstpierpoint, Eng. His infancy was passed amid beautiful surroundings ; and soon his baby feet were chasing butterflies and beetles, and his eager eyes were searching for mosses and flowers. A born naturalist, to the end of his life a new plant, a strange insect, a geological specimen, was of interest ; and any spot " whereon the wild thyme grew " or " the shard-borne beetle wheeled his droning flight," was to his mind a desirable place for a holiday.

The first twelve years of his life were passed at home and in travelling, or in yachting with his father and mother. His education at this time, though broken and desultory, had the advantage of freedom to think for himself, which, with his unusual power of observation, gave him "a sturdy independence of character and a knowledge of men and things quite beyond those of his age." Though never wilfully plotting the same, he was always in mischief, and many are the stories of his fearless and wild adventures. When seven years old he was one day discovered on the topmast of the yacht, suspended on some projection. Again, having acquired the art of making powder squibs, or "blue devils," he sought to "blow up "a wasp's nest, and thereby lost the thumb on his left hand.

At thirteen he entered the Temple School at Brighton, and here his volatile and madcap nature earned for him the title of " Mad Jim ;" but his conscientious truthfulness and trustworthiness made him the favorite with boys and masters. He remained at Brighton only two years, and then left to enter his father's counting-house. Generous, impulsive, and erratic, he was wholly unsuited for a commercial career ; and the record of the six years of his business life show the time to have been filled with more pleasure trips abroad than with work.

March, 1864, Hannington's diary records his commission as second lieutenant in the First Sussex Artillery Volunteers. The year 1868 was eventful to him. On July 5 he received the holy communion for the first time, and on Oct. 22 his name was entered as a commoner in the books of St. Mary Hall, Oxford. Hannington's mind had not been trained to study, and it took him some time to settle down into the course of the university curriculum. He brought much knowledge of the world to Oxford; and this, with his geniality and force of character, made him popular with all classes of fellow-students. His rooms at St. Mary Hall were filled with collections from his wanderings. " Conspicuous was a portrait of his mother, a tall, handsome woman with much facial likeness to her son. "

At times Hannington seemed wholly given over to the spirit of fun ; and his wit was unsparing, yet so good-natured that no one could be vexed with him. He entered heartily into the university sports, and was so much "master of the revels" that it is not surprising the fall of 1869 finds him studying under a private tutor in North Devon, whose cliffs and seas, alas! offered greater distractions even than those of college life.   Returning to Oxford, Hannington, June 12, 1872, took his B. A. degree. Failing in his first examination in September, his ordination did not take place until the end of 1873.   He immediately began his duty as curate of Trentishoe.

The rough work and varied adventures of a Devonshire parish exactly suited Hannington.   In June, 1875, his father proposed to him that he should return to Hurstpierpoint and take charge of St. George; and Aug. 17, with a heavy heart, he said good-by to his Devonshire friends. On Nov. 3, 1875, he received at Oxford his M. A. degree, and on the 7th preached his introductory sermon in St. George's Chapel. Here he labored for seven years, little known to the world, but winning the hearts of his people.

Feb. 10, 1877, James Hannington's marriage with Miss Hankin-Turvin was celebrated. Glimpses into Hannington's diary show records of the increase in the church at Hurst, and mission-work there and in neighboring places. He also speaks of the birth of his two sons and of his daughter, and of growing interest in foreign missions, and of his decision to go into Central Africa under the auspices of the Church Missionary Society. It is impossible to depict the real sorrow of his parishioners, and words cannot convey the heart-anguish felt in his family.

May 17, 1882, Hannington left London in Steamship Quetta in company with other missionaries. They sailed by way of the Mediterranean, and at Aden were transferred into a dirty old vessel called the Mecca, and reached the island of Zanzibar, June 19, in a worn-out condition. The following Sunday evening Mr. Hannington preached in the cathedral. The time at Zanzibar was fully occupied in preparing for the journey into the interior.

The adventures which are now recorded in Hannington's journal are indeed panoramic. July 17 many of the party were stricken with the scourge of African travellers, the dreaded fever. On the 21st the caravan reached a church missionary station, where they were heartily welcomed.

In a short halt near Mpwapwa, Hannington scoured the district to make a collection of its flora and fauna, specimens of which, together with a large collection of birds and insects, he afterwards gave to the British Museum. Aug. 6 Hannington was prostrated with fever; but in the march next day he refused to ride the hospital donkey, and placed instead a weary companion upon the beast. Aug. 30 the party rested at Itura, where the native women, desiring to honor them, executed the national dance. In return, Hannington undressed an English doll before their delighted eyes, and they were charmed with the variety of their white sister's habiliments.

After a long and painful march, interrupted by contact with wild beasts and warlike natives, the caravan arrived at the mission station of Uyui Sept. 4. Here Hannington was seized with dysentery, and for many days hovered between life and death; but, tenderly cared for by his nephew, Gordon, he grew slightly better, and continued the journey in a hammock carried by porters. Nov. 8 the party reached Msalala, and saw at length the waters of the mighty Nyanza.

The rainy season was upon them, and they were obliged to build huts for shelter. Mosquitoes swarmed, lions roared, porters deserted the camp, supplies ran short, and news was received that all were prostrated by fever at Kagei. On Christmas Day the little party was in a state of sad destitution; but, fever-stricken and weary, that band of noble men assembled together to celebrate the holy communion.

Delayed and annoyed by the natives, Hannington at last reached Kagei, Jan. 24, 1883. Here he was welcomed royally by Sayed-ben-Saif, the Arab chief, and encountered friendly Jesuit priests who had recently left Uganda.

After a week's journey, he reached Masalala, to find Mr. Ashe had written thus to the Church Missionary Society : " Hannington is pressing on against all our advice ; if he still lives, I look upon it as your duty to recall him." And so it began to dawn upon his mind that he was beaten, and he consented to try to return to England.

Carried in a hammock by porters, delayed by unfriendly tribes, and sick unto death for a greater part of the way, Hannington reached Zanzibar, May 8, and stood upon the deck of the homeward bound steamer, and June 10, 1883, was again among his friends. " He settled down to his work at Hurst as though he had never left it," but never for a moment lost the idea that he was to renew his labors in Africa. During the next twelve months he preached and spoke upon many platforms.

Near the beginning of 1884 the committee of the Church Missionary Society decided to place the churches of Equatorial

Africa under the supervision of a bishop;
and their eyes naturally turned toward
Hannington, who, with health fully restored, accepted the bishopric as "a sign
from God that he had work to do for
Christ in Africa," and wrote: "I feel that
I could no more say *No* than did Gordon when he went to Khartoum." The
consecration took place June 24, 1884, in
the Parish Church of Lambeth; and, with
the full consciousness that his path would
not be strewn with roses, Hannington went
forth, having arranged that his wife and
her baby, now a few weeks old, should in
time follow him to Africa. Having a commission from the archbishop to visit Jerusalem and confirm the churches on the
way out, he sailed for the Holy Land,
Nov. 5, 1884.

At Jerusalem he inspected, preached,
and confirmed. Jan. 22, the bishop's ship
steams into the harbor of Mombasa. Thousands assembled on shore, and there was a
grand welcome. The whole of the bishop's
working staff consisted of twelve clergy,

priests and deacons, eleven laymen, and five women, wives of missionaries. He at once made himself thoroughly acquainted with all details of his great work. Finding the missionaries dwelling in "houses of cedar, while the ark scarce rested in curtains," the bishop wrote to the committee at once for a new church — "not a tin ark or cocoanut barn, but a proper stone church, a church to the glory of God."

With regard to the marriage question the bishop wrote: "It is homicide to permit young married women to go beyond the neighborhood of the coast, and *nothing shall* induce me to give my consent that ladies should attempt to cross the Wanyamnezi deserts in the present state of the country."

Before he had been long living in Frere Town famine threatened the mission station at Taita. He determined that he would himself go to the front to carry supplies to Mr. Wray's suffering camp. The heat was intense, and the journey marked by dangers of all kinds; but the bishop's party at last reached Taita, and, finding the station demoralized by famine and privation, transferred the band to Rabai. In due time the bishop brought his whole party safely through to Rabai, but he himself pushed straight on to Frere Town, having had a tramp of five hundred miles. He was filled with joy and enthusiasm over the new route westward, which was free from the malarial scourge that had accompanied his terrible march from Zanzibar to the lake the previous year.

In May, 1885, Bishop Hannington wrote the committee of the Church Missionary Society of his determination to travel westward across the terrible Masai country, and thereby to open a new route to the lake. His plans were well laid, and bravely and successfully carried out; but, alas! neither he nor his advisers knew the terrible fact that Mtèsa was dead, and that the young king, Mwanga, had ordered the death sentence for all white men who should enter Uganda through the northeast. And so, July 23, 1885, after prodigious labors in

preparation, Hannington again led the way
into the wilds of darkest Africa, at the
head of a caravan two hundred strong.

Letters home, and the pocket diary, recovered by a Christian lad, give the bishop's own record of forty-mile marches
under the burning sun, of paths cut
through a tangle of spiked grasses, of
jungles filled with wild beasts, of hostile
tribes, and at last of the terrible Masai.
"Starvation, desertion, treachery," and
other nightmares and furies, did, indeed,
hover over their heads in ghostly forms,
but all were met and conquered with
indomitable courage; and Oct. 11, 1885,
the bishop arrived at Kwa Sundu. Here
he decided to leave the caravan with the
native clergyman, Mr. Jones; and, select-
ing fifty men to accompany him, pushed
on to the lake.

It was truly a march of death, for, Oct.
21, 1885, the bishop was captured by
Lubwa's band, and, after an imprisonment
of seven days filled with exquisite torture,
he was led out and brutally murdered

within two days' march of his heart's long-cherished dream, the land of the Uganda.

Since the death of David Livingstone, the great missionary and explorer, the cause of missions in the Dark Continent has suffered no greater loss than in the untimely death of the brilliant and intrepid missionary, Bishop Hannington, at the early age of thirty-eight.

XXIII.

DAVID LIVINGSTONE.

Missionary to Africa.

BORN MARCH 19, 1813; DIED MAY 1, 1873.

DAVID LIVINGSTONE.

XXIII.

DAVID LIVINGSTONE.

THE visitor in Westminster Abbey, after looking at the royal tombs in the Chapel of Henry VII., and inspecting with nearer interest the tablets and monuments of the famous Poets' Corner, may come out into the great nave of the cathedral, and there, apart from the other famous graves, but, as it were, nearer to the people and even amid them, in the middle of the floor he finds the large slab which bears the name of David Livingstone. Livingstone was certainly not a literary man in the common meaning, though his works hold an important place in English literature; he was certainly not a mere geographical explorer, though no name among the explorers honored by the Royal Geographical Society can compare with his; and mis-

sionaries and directors of missionary work
were not quite sure whether he could
stand among them. In 1856 the London Missionary Society seemed "desirous
of shelving his plans; so he shelved the
society." Yet Livingstone, in 1865, after
he had been ten years independent of the
missionary society, declined Sir Roderick
Murchison's tempting invitation to be a
mere explorer, and insisted, as he had
from the beginning, that "The end of the
geographical feat is but the beginning
of the missionary enterprise." However
others might misunderstand him, in his
own mind he was always the missionary
explorer and pioneer; the greatest missionary pioneer he really was since the
Apostle Paul.

He was born at Blantyre, near Glasgow,
Scotland, March 19, 1813, the son of
"poor and pious parents," as he himself
wrote on their tombstone, giving thanks
for their poverty as well as their piety.
When nine years old he took a prize for
repeating Psalm cxix., "with only two

errors." When but ten he went to work in a cotton factory, and laid his first half-crown of wages in his mother's lap, and with part of that week's pay bought a Latin grammar. For ten years he studied late at night, and at odd minutes in the mill, and read many of the classics. Till about 1833 he was waiting for some gracious, conscious change to come in his character, but, reading Dick's " Philosophy of a Future State," he was led to accept Christ at once with great joy; and Gutzlaff's " Appeal " led him to give himself to missionary work.

He spent two winters (1836–38) in Glasgow, studying Greek in the University, theology with Rev. Dr. Wardlaw, and medicine in Anderson's College; and was accepted by the London Missionary Society to go to China, and at their instance studied theology for a time with the Rev. Richard Cecil, though poor reports of his preaching capacity nearly caused his rejection by the society.

His going to China was delayed by the

opium war; and meeting Moffat, he concluded to go to Africa. He received a
medical diploma, and was ordained in November, 1840, and in December sailed for
the Cape; and in July, 1841, went to
Kuruman, Moffat's station, seven hundred
miles north of Cape Town. He spent two
years at Kuruman, learning the language
and practical missionary methods; and in
1843 established his own first station at
Mabotsa, two hundred miles north-east of
Kuruman, where he built a house, and took
home Mary Moffat as his wife.

His plan was to open up new centres
of light among tribes hitherto unevan-
gelized, and raise up native pastors. He
had no patience with lingering near the
centres of missionary or civilized life.
"If you meet me down in the Colony
before eight years are expired," he wrote
to a friend, "you may shoot me." Near
Mabotsa, before his marriage, he had the
famous encounter with a lion, which bit
through his arm bone. Some one in
London asked him what his thoughts were

as the lion stood over him ; and he answered with grim humor, " I was thinking
what part of me he would eat first."

He had built his house to stay at Mabotsa ; but a foolish jealousy on the part
of a fellow missionary made him give
up his home, and found a second station
forty miles north, at Chonuane, the capital
of the Bakwains. Here he labored three
years, and the chief, Sechéle, was baptized;
but the people suffered from drought, and
their "rain-makers" charged it to the
missionary. Livingstone thereupon per-
suaded the tribe to move westward forty
miles to the river Kolobeng, where canals
could furnish irrigation. This "beat the
rain-makers" for the first year ; but later
droughts showed the river insufficient, and
in 1849, leaving his wife and three children at Kolobeng, he set out in company
with two English sportsmen, to find the
tribe a healthier home to the north. He
discovered Lake 'Ngami, Aug. 1 ; then returned, and the next April set out to
occupy it with his wife and children and

the converted chief Sechéle. The children and servants, however, fell ill, and he had to return. A fourth child was born and died ere long; and after fuller preparation he again set out with his family, in April, 1851, for the country of the Makololo, whose king, Sebituane, had been in former years a good friend of Sechéle. This time the journey was successfully accomplished, and Sebituane welcomed them heartily. He soon died; but his daughter, who succeeded him, was equally friendly, and Livingstone continued his explorations, and in June discovered the upper Zambesi.

The Makololo country, however, was not healthful, and the political disorders and strife with the Boers made Kolobeng unsafe; and in 1852 Livingstone took his family to the Cape, and sent them to England, himself returning to the Makololo.

In November, 1853, he set out with a company of natives upon that great exploring tour which led him north-westerly across the watershed of Central Africa, and brought him, in May, 1854, to the Portuguese town of Loanda on the west coast. Here he rested through the summer, and in September following marched eastward, and explored across the continent from ocean to ocean, reaching the mouth of the Zambesi in May, 1856.

He had sent home from Loanda his astronomical observations and his journals to that point ; and the Royal Geographical Society honored him in May, 1855, with its gold medal. His careful studies of the watershed on his eastward journey were of equal value. He discovered the great falls of the Zambesi, and the blank, " unexplored region " from Kuruman to Timbuctoo was covered with his accurate and scientific descriptions and maps ; and when from Kilimane he sailed to Mauritius, and thence to England, where he arrived in December, 1856, he was the hero of the hour. His journey of eleven thousand miles through unexplored Africa had brought him into national and world-wide distinction. His meeting with his family was a greater joy than all his fame, though he found his father's chair empty, Neil Livingstone having died while his son was on his homeward journey.

The London Missionary Society gave him distinguished honor, but doubted the entire wisdom of his plans; and he resigned his connection with them. He prepared and published his first volume, "Missionary Travels and Researches in South Africa," which had an immediate popular success, and made him pecuniarily independent. Eminent scientists pronounced it a most valuable contribution to knowledge. It gave a most interesting proof of his personal traits. For example, in describing in the simplest manner an adventure with a buffalo, he says: —

"I glanced around, but the only tree on the plain was a hundred yards off, and there was no escape elsewhere. I therefore cocked my rifle with the intention of giving him a steady shot in the forehead when he should come within three or four yards of me. The thought flashed across my mind, 'What if the gun misses fire?' I placed it at my shoulder as he came on at full speed, and that is

ɑemendous. A small bush fifteen yards off made
him swerve a little, and exposed his shoulder. I
heard the ball crack there as I fell flat on my face.
The pain must have made him renounce his purpose, for he bounded close past me to the water,
where he was found dead. In expressing my thankfulness to God among my men, they were much
offended with themselves for not being present to
shield me from this danger. The tree near me was
a camel-thorn, and reminded me that we had come
back to the land of thorns again, for the country we
had left is one of evergreens."

The passage, besides its graphic interest,
shows Livingstone's coolness in the moment of danger, his devout thankfulness
and habit of speaking of God's kind providences to his men, whom he held in
friendly regard, and the keen eye of the
naturalist noting even the thorns on the
bush in the moment of deadly danger.

But, above all, his book reveals his con-
trolling and devoted purpose of missionary
exploration ; and more and more the Christian church grows to see the justice of its
ideas of missionary work. Especially was
it wise in declaring the slave-trade the

great " open sore of the world," which, un-
healed, must make the Christianization or
civilizing of Africa an impossibility.

In February, 1858, he was appointed
British consul for Eastern Africa and the
interior, and in March sailed· in the Zambesi expedition. He explored the Zambesi from its mouth that season, entered
its branch, the Shiré, in January, 1859, and
discovered Lake Nyassa Sept. 16, 1859.
He was joined by the Oxford and Cam-
bridge missionaries early in 1861 ; explored
with them the Rovuma, and later again explored the Shiré. Jan. 30, 1862, Mrs.
Livingstone came to join him, arriving in
the naval ship Gorgon, which also brought
a small steamer, the Lady Nyassa, which,
at the cost of six thousand pounds, profits
of his book, he had had built for lake
use.

Mrs. Livingstone died April 27, and at
first he was quite prostrated. Later he
again explored the Rovuma and Shiré Rivers, and had begun to build a road around
the cataracts of the latter river, when letters

were received from England, recalling the
expedition as too costly. The recall was in
part due to the hostility of the Portuguese
authorities, because of his practical interference with the slave-trade.

In need now of money, he sailed his
little steamer, the Lady Nyassa, to Bombay,
to sell her, making a stormy journey of
forty-five days ; and from Bombay sailed to
England. There he wrote, " The Zambesi
and its Tributaries."

In 1865 Sir Roderick Murchison proposed to him to accept a purely geographical appointment, to explore the watersheds
of Africa ; but Livingstone declined, being
unwilling to put the missionary work anywhere but first. This refusal did not prevent his appointment as British consul in
Africa, without salary ; and he accepted this
office, and also a commission from the Geo-
grapical Society, under which he went to
Bombay and sold the Lady Nyassa for less
than half her cost to him, thence sailing
to Zanzibar, whence he went to the mouth
of the Rovuma. He had already ascer-

tained that this river had no connection
with Lake Nyassa, but he ascended it as
far as practicable, and reached Lake Nyassa
Aug. 8, spending some weeks in exploring the lake; and then, to settle the question of the watershed, he pressed on
northward, and reached Lake Tanganyika
April 1, 1867, and demonstrated that it belonged to a system of waters flowing away
from the Indian Ocean. Then, pushing
west, he came to Casembe in November,
discovering Lake Moero, Nov. 8, 1867.

These laborious journeys were most
wearing to his health, and he was prostrated
by a severe fever in December, and Jan. 1,
1868, wrote in his journal: " Almighty
Father, forgive the sins of the past year
for thy Son's sake. Help me to be more
profitable during this year. If I am to die
this year, prepare me for it." This danger
of death and these laborious journeys were
for no mere explorer's fame. They were
the steadfast persistence of his great purpose to accomplish the " geographical feat,"
which was " but the beginning of the mis-

sionary enterprise ; " along with which was
now his purpose to find and show, north of
the Portuguese possessions, and Portuguese official complicity with the slave-
trade, an open highway of legitimate
commerce, the success of which he was
convinced would ever heal " the open sore
of the world."

Yet he ever bore with him the fitting influence of a devoted missionary of the
cross. In the midst of these geographical
explorations, while reaching the conclusion
that Lake Bangweolo, discovered July 28,
1868, was one of a chain of lakes extending northward and traversed by the Lualaba, and wondering if that mighty interior
river was not the long-sought upper Nile,
he makes this note : " As for our general
discourse, we mention our relationship to
our Father; his love to all his children —
the guilt of selling any of his children,
the consequence. We mention the Bible,
future state, prayers ; advise union, that they
should unite as one family to expel enemies, who came first as slave-traders, and

ended by leaving the country a wilderness."

Toward the end of 1868 he was again very ill ; and at length resolved to go to Ujiji, on the east shore of Lake Tanganyika. The journey was most exhausting. Half-way to Tanganyika he became so ill that he had to be carried on the march — the first time in thirty years. His, men, too were about worn out. Canoeing on the lake was easier than marching, but taxed them to the utmost. " Patience," he says, " was never more needed than now. I am near Ujiji ; but the slaves who paddle are tired, and no wonder ; they keep up a roaring song all through their work, night and day. . . . Hope to hold out to Ujiji." They arrived there March 14, 1869.

It was July before Livingstone was sufficiently rested and strengthened to set out on what proved his last journey. His immediate object was the exploration of that country west from the northern land of Lake Tanganyika. The country was said to be occupied by cannibals ; but beyond

them was the Lualaba, and the question
whether it flowed northward to the Nile
was of intense interest. He found the people drunken with palm-toddy, and obsti-
nately obstructive to him. After a short
attempt at canoeing on the Lualaba, his ill-
health compelled falling back to Bambarré
by the lake. In June, 1870, he made another start, but again had to fall back, and
was laid up nearly three months with ulcers
on his feet. He says that while in this
country he " read the whole Bible through
four times." He confessed in his journal :
" I have an intense and sore longing to
finish and retire, and trust the Almighty
may permit me to go home."

Jan. 1, 1871, he was still waiting at
Bambarré. There ten men came of a
larger number sent from Zanzibar by Dr.
Kirk, but bringing only one of the forty
letters with which they had been sent, and
proving most mutinous, worthless scoun-
drels when he tried to go westward with
them. Nevertheless, he pushed on to the
Lualaba, but found it wandering off still

westward, apparently with no connection
with the Nile.   Here, too, he had to witness, with no power to help, the horror and
desolation of a slavers' raid, with all its
robbery, massacre, and utter desolation.
Obliged to return, he came east six hundred miles to Ujiji, to find that there his
stores had been stolen, and he was threatened with utter destitution.   This was Oct.
23, 1871 ; and it was in this extremity that
he was relieved by the arrival of Henry M.
Stanley, of the *New York Herald* relief
expedition, Nov. 10.

In September, 1866, men whom Livingstone had brought from Zanzibar deserted
him, and in order to get pay on the arrival
there, represented that he had been killed
by the natives.   The report was discred-
ited, but years without messages made it
seem not improbable.   The Geographical
Society commissioned Mr. Edward D.
Young to search for Livingstone, and he
proved the utter untrustworthiness of the
report.   But what truth was hidden in
these dark and trackless forests it was left

to Stanley to show, after an anxious uncertainty of years. Stanley brought with him abundant equipment; and he and Livingstone together explored the north end of Lake Tanganyika, and found that it had no northern outlet, and so could not be a source of the Nile. Subsequently Stanley was prostrated with fever; and for this and other causes he was with Livingstone till the middle of February, 1872. It belongs to Henry M. Stanley to tell how much of all that is noblest in him has its connection with that heroic missionary whom the *New York Herald's* enterprise sent him out to rescue.

They went together to Unyanyembe, a great Arab settlement between Ujiji and the east coast. There Stanley handed over the stores he had brought for Livingstone, public gifts, and clothing sent by his daughter; and after they had shaken hands and parted, sent up from the coast a company of trusty natives.

Aug. 25 Livingstone left Unyanyembe, and in six weeks was back at Lake Tanganyika.   He rounded the southern point, and pushed south and west for Lake Bangweolo.   The rainy season had come ; and they were much hindered by the " sponge," and were often knee-deep in water.   Fever and dysentery reduced Livingstone, till again he had to be carried on a sort of palanquin.   Sometimes he was in great pain, and sometimes faint and drowsy.   He kept up his journal ; but the entries were shorter and shorter, at last little but the dates.   He still questioned the men, where he could not observe for himself, about distant hills and the rivers they crossed.   April 27, 1873, he wrote, " Knocked up quite, and remain — recover — sent to buy milch goats.   We are on the banks of Molilamo."   This was the last entry.

Next day his men lifted him from his bed to a canoe, and crossed the river. They then bore him to the site of the present village of Chitambo, at the southern end of Lake Bangweolo, reaching there with great difficulty, splashing through dreary stretches of water and sponge till the evening of April 29. He was at times utterly faint. Some of them went ahead, and built him a hut, and there they laid him in bed. Next day he was too ill to talk. At night they helped him select some medicine from the chest. Then he said, "All right; you can go." A lad slept in the hut with him, and towards morning called some of the men. They found his candle burning at his bedside, and Livingstone kneeling there as if in prayer, his face in his hands, but he was dead.

When these poor natives found that " the great master," as they called him, was dead, " with a fidelity which is rare in story, and a sense of responsibility almost unknown in benighted Africa," they buried his heart and internal organs under a tree — Livingstone wrote after his wife's death, " I have often wished that [my resting-place] might be in some far-off, still, deep forest, where I may sleep sweetly till the resurrection morn." His body they embalmed, as best they could, by drying; and wrapping it in calico, bark, and canvas, carried it, with all his personal effects, through a hostile country, all the weary way to the coast. It was thence taken to England, and there identified, partly by the arm crushed by the lion's jaw; and was laid to rest in Westminster Abbey.

GAYLORD

PRINTED IN U.S.A